MACRAMÉ FOR BEGINNERS

A step by step guide to learn the macrame art. Make your handmade unique with illustrated knots patterns and give a stylish touch to your home

OLYVIA SHIRLEY

Summary

INTRODUCTION

Macramé is a type of decorative knot that can be found in almost every culture, but it takes on different forms in different cultures. Knot-tying is mainly performed by youth scouts and cadets, particularly in second-cycle institutions as part of their training sessions.

After its formal introduction as a topic in various universities, macramé art has grown in popularity. It's now used in conjunction with other materials to create a wide range of beautiful works of art. Macramé is closely correlated with fashionable teenagers due to its fast development, great adaptability, and wide range of applications. Macramé is a common fashion decoration that emerged in Eastern textiles and developed into a key component in the development of each decorative garment, especially at the tent, garment, and towel fringes.

Macramé is an Italian term used in Genoa. It became the most popular textile technique in conventional ways. Knots is used for a number of mnemonics, utilitarian, and superstitious purposes over time, and knotting emerged in early Egyptian culture in Africa, where knots were used in fishnet and decorative fringes. The Quipu, made of mnemonic knots (overhand knots), was used by the Incas of Peru to record and convey knowledge.

The use of knots, their shape, the colour of a rope, and the knot itself all contributed to the complex meanings being conveyed. Knots were used in medicine (as slings for broken bones) and sports in ancient Greece, such as the Gordian knot, which was one such mystery. Both early Egyptians and Greeks used the 'Hercules' knot (square knot) on clothing, jewels, and pottery with magical or religious connotations.

While macramé art has been created and used for further development in most cultures to achieve both functional and artistic appeal, the final products differ depending on the culture. The ornamental usage of knotting separates early cultures and reflects intellectual growth. It is an art for people of all ages and skills. Today, Macramé is commemorating the twentieth-century revival. 'Men and women work with their hands to produce utilitarian and aesthetic objects. Despite its importance, macramé is regarded as merely a shape knotting technique due to its simplicity and versatility. Although its value, macramé as a knotting technique is limited by its simplicity and current usability. Macramé is a vibrant, adaptable, and exploratory material that lends itself to processing and handling in product production and manufacturing in a variety of ways. Macramé has been a highly prized talent all over the world since its conception.

In the 13th century, the invention of macramé passed through Arabia. Spain spread to the rest of Europe after the Moorish invasion of Turkey in the early 14th century, arriving in Italy and France in the early 14th and 15th centuries, and was later adopted into England in the late 17th century and mid-to-late 19th century during the Victorian era.

Historians and sailors are said to have disseminated this form of art around the world. Macramé had entered its dormant phase in China and America by the 1920s, when it was used to make objects such as flower hangers, expertly made belts, and industrial containers.

Macramé has also shown to be a perfect herbal therapy for people seeking detox procedures, and it aims to boost memories once again, making it a wonderful experience for everyone. Rope play and tying protects the hands and limbs while loosening the wrist and finger joints.

It will help calm the mind and spirit because it needs concentration, and the repetitive patterns will place a weaver in a meditative state. Also, stress is believed to be released by the fingertips, making macramé knotting a pleasurable experience. Macramé has the added benefit of enjoying the self-expression process by creating the intrinsic target concealed within.

CHAPTER ONE

History Of Macramé And Its Benefits

Macramé's Origin

Macramé is the art of tying knots to create delicate formed textiles. Many people claim that the word macramé came from the Arabic word "migramah," which means "fringe." Back in the 13th century, Arabic weavers used macramé to create fashionable fringes, shawls, and veils. Others, on the other hand, say that knot-tying dates back to the third century in China. Lanterns, ritual robes, and hangings from this time period feature intricate knots, and the classic pan chang knot is considered an ancient form of macramé by others.

Europe to Africa

The origins of macramé are unclear, although it is widely assumed that the Moors were responsible for spreading the art. During their travels from North Africa to Europe, the Moors brought macramé to Spain, where it spread to France in the fifteenth century and Italy in the sixteenth. From there, macramé spread across Europe. Later in the seventeenth century, Queen Mary II of England takes a personal interest in the art. She taught it to her waitresses as well.

By sea if not by land

The Moors, on the other hand, were not only advocates for Macramé. It was common among European sailors, who used it to save time at sea during the long months by tying knots on a regular basis. On voyages dating back to the nineteenth century, British and American sailors traded and priced macramé pieces they had made. When making knotted things like hammocks and ties, it's known as "square knotting" or macramé.

The Hobby of a Homemaker

In Victorian England, macramé was at its peak. Several teen girls were taught macramé as part of their schooling to become women, a common practise among women. Magazines and home publications provided advice on everything from macramé tablecloths to macramé curtains. Macramé could be used in nearly any trendy home's interior.

A Craze from the 70s

Macramé dropped out of favour in the twentieth century before making a return in the 1970s, when it became the go-to fabric for interior design and clothing. Plant hangers, vests, furniture, ties, and bikinis were all made of Macramé. The New York Times also included a Christmas Tree macramé in 1976. Unfortunately, the craze was short-lived:

by the 1980s, macramé had disappeared from popularity. Macramé is making a comeback, thanks to social media. It's a must-have for any boho or new room, and it's commonly used to make plant hangers and wall hangings. It's not only different from the prints, but it's also a lot of fun to look at. However, if you're thinking of bringing together a macramé tree, you may be on your own.

Crafting for Mental Wellbeing, Art as Counseling, Macramé, and us.

Humankind has been questioning the concept of art since the dawn of human history. For Tolstoy, art served as a bridge of empathy between ourselves and others, and for Anas Nin, it served as a way of exorcising our moral surplus. But something that reconciles the two may be the biggest artistic achievement: a conduit of empathy within our mind that allows us to exorcise and truly appreciate our emotions, in other words, a form of therapy.

Wow, Macramé has done it. It's just part of the creative process, which is ongoing at various times. Beginner macramé creators, as well as experts, can find it soothing, fun, artistic, and satisfying. There are an increasing number of choices for great macramé to complement the décor of your home, personal style, and clothing for those who simply want to use and enjoy the finished pieces.

Macramé's talent and hobby today mean very different things to many people; for others, the gift is excellent and unique in many ways, while for others, it makes no difference. Macramé involves tying knots, which strengthens the hands and muscles. Making a macramé product can be very calming and soothing for the body, soul, and mind; it is also an eco-sustainable art option. These are only a few of the benefits that Macramé art enthusiasts believe this art form provides to its practitioners.

Macramé and the various decorative items and useful products it manufactures have added benefits. Macramé is a natural therapy. The strings' pulling and functioning tend to stabilise the hands and limbs. It helps in joint lubrication. Some people discover that macramé is a meditative art form in which repetitive knots are used to create patterns that promote relaxation. A hobbyist simply needs some twine and a few basic knots to explore the immense potential of macramé. Macramé is an art that does not need a lot of different materials or supplies. Macramé is making a comeback in a big way.

The art of knotting a series of abstract shapes without the use of knots, chains, or needles is referred to as macramé.

Macramé has been around since the 13th century. The word "macramé" comes from the Arabic word "fringe." Arabian weavers are thought to have begun the skill by knotting extra material at the sides of loamed material. At the beginning of the fourteenth and fifteenth centuries, it effectively transported it from these sources to Italy and France. Sailors learned the art because it was a fun way to pass the time while serving at sea. Sailing knots include the half knot, half-hitch knot, and square knot, which are today's simple macramé knots. The sailors turned over their craft to the Chinese, who put it to use in their own civilization and culture. The British developed a taste for talent in the nineteenth century.

When time passed, the powers faded into obscurity. It was revived in the 1960s and 1970s, and it possessed the ancient force of rejuvenation. The interest of macramé waned in the 1980s and 1990s, but it resurfaced in full force at the turn of the twenty-first century, with an endless variety of creative possibilities for the hobbyist, appreciator, and designer among the many different pieces of macramé.

Macramé is a passion and a skill that means different things to different people these days. The talent is fantastic in many ways for many people. Hands and arms may be strengthened by tying a variety of knots. Building a macramé project can be very calming for the body, mind, and spirit. Macramé designs need few machinery and resources that are free of additives and fumes; it is unquestionably an environmentally friendly, natural skill.

Macramé accessories, macramé plant hangers and wall hangers, handbags and ties, and home decorations are all examples of designs. The various shades and textures of macramé have a wide variety of options. The fabrics range from various thicknesses of jute and hemp to twin, polyester fibres, and dyed nylon. You may use wooden beads in your designs, but ceramic and glass beads are also common these days.

Art, like all other instruments, will help us extend our ability beyond what we were born with. In this case of the mind rather than the body, art compensates for inborn flaws, flaws that we might refer to as psychological frailties.

Additional Advantages of the Macramé Pattern

Pattern appeals to teenagers because it motivates them to create spectacular creations that they can use to showcase or demonstrate their imagination to friends. They want to create exclusive items, such as friendship bands and bracelets, to distribute at markets or as gifts.

Summertime is the best time to wear Macramé bracelets and anklets. They're not only great for the best, but they're also great for the pool. They are relatively easy to obtain for female-gender girls. The following are ideas for young people to consider as they plan their summer projects, including a macramé template to wear.

Macramé is looking for patterns to create as items for this medium of art. The type of jute almond or cotton, for example, could determine the types of problems as well as the colours of the falls used to produce the cable usage design. The cable tones will also help to improve the falls, bracelets, and changes. Once you've stored or sorted the materials in plastic containers, make sure you label them properly.

The first step was to prepare for the possibility of pattern formation. Adults may guide the youth in selecting a pattern, and they may also end up in a craft store.

When purchasing the required macramé pattern, adults may assist a young person in deciding on the pattern. In addition, the children's supply or the base measurement measures; this is paramount throughout the piece. Build the cable up to 7 or 8 times longer due to the difficulties and splits.

Children will find the knot that will be the most difficult to undo, particularly when creating basic designs. It's often done this way, because it's a really simple approach with just four patterns. The concept could be turned to avoid it rotating if desired. If the definition requires a spinning wire, however, use one-not simply for the same function. The pattern would be pressured as a result of this.

Between issue sequences, youth can find two falls. They could put a ring in the middle of the package. Approximate this position or, as a result, like the links for that falls after about 20 problems. The youth-created macramé software will be used in the Drops Room.

They must learn to tidy up after themselves and return objects to their correct storage areas as quickly as possible. Trash should surely be disposed of properly. Macramé pattern-making in this manner is not only a social interaction in which young people can form bonds and demonstrate excellent support, but it is also an enjoyable activity.

WHAT IS MACRAMÉ

Macramé is a form of textile production that does not use the traditional methods of weaving or knitting, instead relying on a series of knots. It is said to have begun in the western hemisphere in the 13th century with all of the Arab weavers. Some remaining ribbons or fibres from the ends of all hand-woven cloths, such as blankets, veils, and shawls, are not to be made into decorative fringes. What we find interesting is that the sailors were the ones who genuinely developed this appeal and were then criticised for disseminating it to different states through the vents where it would eventually end. They used the handles of knives, bottles, and other objects found on the boat to decorate them and use them to find whatever they needed or wished when they got ashore. In reaction to this, 19th-century sailors used a method known as "square foot" to make hammocks and straps.

Cotton wool, hemp, rope, or leather are popular materials for macramé. The square knot, which has complete viability, and the double half hitch are the main knots, though there are variants. Ribbons are often combined with diamonds, rings, or cubes to create jewellery. If you look at the vast majority of friendship bracelets worn by college students, you'll notice that they're made of macramé.

Macramé's popularity waned for a while, but it was revived in the 1970s by American neo-hippies and grunge audiences, who used it to make jewellery. Handmade bracelets, anklets, and bracelets is embellished with handmade glass beads and natural elements like shell and bone.

Macramé is a fun craft to try, and you can get started with very little money. You could come across a lot of low-cost or no-cost templates available, as well as a few excellent how-to books to get you started. This may be an excellent activity to keep your children, grandchildren, or someone else occupied.

Because of its feasibility, this approach would most certainly be open to some extent. Surprisingly, making something with just your hands and inexpensive materials is very possible.

Macramé is a fabric-making technique that employs a large number of knots to achieve a simple shape and function. Every can be made entirely with your hands, and no instruments are needed apart from a routine ring to hold the product in place as you exercise.

To consider macramé, the project must have at least one macramé knot. Macramé activities are usually pieced together with a lot of knots. Macramé elements are occasionally paired with other methods such as pruning or knitting.

Macramé is a flexible fibre item that can be used to create anything from figurines to jewellery, luggage, and clothes. Embellishments like wooden or glass beads, when mixed with colourful threads, will open up a world of possibilities.

Learn a little about the fascinating history of macramé before moving on to the basic techniques and advice for finding the best way to start making your own macramé.

Macramé is essentially textile fabrics that have been knotted together. There are several different kinds of knots that can be used to make macramé, ranging from simple to complicated. Apart from the fact that commercial businesses need devices such as mounting rings, you can tie the knots with your fingertips. That's how easy it is to make. You may explore it while sitting at home or, more possibly, bored at work. To be called macramé, anything must have a simple knot structure. Some methods, such as stitching and knitting, are used in some macramé fabrics.

The "reef knot," or what we like to call a square macramé, hitches and half hitches, is a more common macramé pattern. This were designed by sailors who wanted to make decorative knots that could be worn or used to decorate interior spaces. It was also required to secure their knives, bottles, and ship components. Leather belts and other styles of cloth are often made using macramé techniques.

Macramé can also be used to make bracelets, jewellery, and decorative items. In the 1970s, macramé gained popularity. You can guess how long this piece of art has been around. It joins embroidery, quilting, and needlework as ancient crafts. In both of these, macramé seems to be the only genre of art that is currently undergoing a revival. While cotton and wool are the most common plant fibres used in macramé, other materials such as glasses and dyed threads can be added to give it a more trendy and impressive look.

BENEFITS OF MACRAMÉ

• Physical Health Benefits

The indoor garden will provide a safe refuge from the outside world, as well as a source of great enjoyment for many people. If you incorporate those plants into your home, whether you live in a small bedroom or a large house, you will begin to feel safer and notice positive and rewarding improvements. Using various colours of macramé plant hangers will enhance the overall attractiveness of your garden area, living space, and patios outdoors. Plants and macramé work together to boost mood and create a comfortable living environment, which can also assist with loneliness and depression. Caring for a living being provides purpose and satisfaction, particularly when you see a lovely macramé plant hanger blooming and thriving in its new home.

Youth love the template because it allows them to make a variety of decisions while also allowing them to create stunning patterns that they are excited to show off to their peers at a later date. We all enjoy designing creative items, such as anklets that mimic bracelets and unity bands, which we can sell or give away as gifts.

• Crafting for Mental Health

Today, Macramé is a passion and a talent that means a variety of different things to different people; in some ways, the expertise is brilliant and special, while for others, it doesn't matter. Macramé is the art of tying knots to help you balance your arms and hands. Macramé is a great way to unwind and heal the body. Making a macramé product also relaxes the mind and soul, and it's an environmentally conscious art style. There are only a handful of the benefits for those who do it.

There are several benefits of macramé, in addition to the numerous novelty products and useful items it produces. It is mainly used for medicinal purposes. Pulling and twisting strings serves to stabilise the hands and body. Macramé also promotes joint loosening. Macramé, which is a meditative art of repeated knots used to create shapes, is considered by others to be meditative and to add peace and calm to the mind. A hobbyist just requires a few twines and a few basic knots to explore the vast possibilities that macramé has to offer. Macramé art does not necessitate a large number of products or tools.

• Wellbeing

In a society where so much of our work is intangible, where occupations and culture are often separated, and where science is conducted on machines and in the modern world, doing things with our hands and fingertips gives us a sense of strength and superiority. This is a way of creating tangible balance and beauty, a real sensory touchpoint, and reintroducing a sense of free and relaxed play into our productive adult lives. Too much so that many experts are now recommending knitting as a form of therapy. Knitting, crocheting, sewing, and Macramé all have a healing experience, and the community has come to recognise this.

• It Serves as a Relaxation Therapy

Knitting, crocheting, sewing, and Macramé all have a healing experience, and the community has come to recognise this.

In today's world, stress therapy is causing a lot of debate. With so many events on the rise and so many people's busy lives, it's more important than ever to find equilibrium through acts that relax the emotions and relieve anxiety. Some mental issues that need serious treatment include depression and anxiety. All of these are the product of the body's reaction to such incidents and casualties. Macramé art is an excellent way to relieve tension. The processes involved in making macramé art divert your mind away from the tension and mental imbalances that your body is experiencing and instead concentrate it on the craft. The satisfaction of having to make something beautiful is a healthy way to relieve tension.

• It Strengthens Your Arms

Strengthen the limbs and muscles by tying macramé knots and designs. Macramé knot tying will be used to restore resilience to people who have started to experience symptoms that weaken their arms and muscles. If you begin to tie and knot, you will see a gradual reduction in your discomfort and muscle contractions. You'll probably notice that the joints are getting more open and loose.

• Macramé Is Extremely Therapeutic

The "Relaxation Response" is described as "rhythmic repetitive movements that seem to place us in the present moment, calming our heads, which are so often full of activity and worries," and the study indicates that such repeated actions, such as coming from our hands and moving from side to side with our pupils, have a strong soothing effect.

Knitting necessitates a complex, simultaneous, and coordinated action phase, as well as a significant amount of brain activity, so that the brain has less time to pay attention to those problems, and it's an excellent soothing strategy for those suffering from chronic pain. Knitting also improves serotonin development, which can help us feel more comfortable and happy. The calming rhythmic nature of the movements leads to a contemplative mood.

Knitting transports you to a peaceful, quiet spot where the pattern and stitches are all you can think about. You can feel the texture of the fabric, see the bright colours, hear the needles continuously turning, and feel a sense of pride for the dream concept and the final product. The different odours in all-natural goat wool can be detected. Time begins to slow down while much of this is heard. Your worries are increasingly dissipating. And the sense of pride you get when you do something is unrivalled.

• Medical Benefits

A well-known psychotherapist discovered through studies that there is still a need for an entire-person approach to psychological therapy through medical practise, and that the cycle of true healing emanates from deep inside the mind and spirit and can occur even though a "cure" is not present. Therapeutic spinning can be used to improve health and safety. It can benefit those who are suffering from pain, stress, or other mental health issues.

• Connects Us

Knitting also connects you to a social network and fellow knitter's mates, which is especially true for someone who feels isolated, depressed, and lonely, among other physical health benefits such as being a pain reliever and stress reliever. Knitters build things that people admire. You can make yourself feel comfortable by stroking wool like a knitter. Knitting and crocheting are the one basic soothing and relaxing device that you can bring with you everywhere you go to get peace of mind and a lovely scarf.

MACRAMÉ APPLICATIONS

• Every Day Uses of Macramé

When it comes to interior decorating, macramé projects have a wide range of uses. Macramé has been discovered to give the houses, workplaces, and halls a trendy and appropriate appearance. It's an excellent choice for hanging, wrapping, and storing objects because of the many variations that can be made for it. It can be built to work with other things and objects. If you're looking for a fresh look for your shopping mall or want to add a bit of class and sophistication to your house, macramé is a perfect option. We've compiled a list of some of the most popular ways macramé can be used today.

• Macramé Tapestry

The installation of a macramé tapestry to your home would certainly bring charm and sophistication. When you investigate the parts of your home and walls that seem to be bland and uninteresting. Tapestry is a nice way to adjust what you see in the overview box. In the bedroom and living room, these patterns could be hung over the headboards of beds and sofas. You could tie the tapestry to a wooden and slender branch of a tree to give the eyes a more realistic and vegetative appearance. The macramé tapestry pattern may not sag as a result of this addition. When anything sags, it loses its balance and location in the places of the house where it was previously placed. Macramé wall arts, it has been observed, really bring out the artistic beauty of the craft.

• Dreamcatchers

A macramé dream catcher is a beautiful way to teach guests a lot about the house and family they've just entered. You will do this to help visitors feel more at ease and open up to you. Peace, restfulness, and positivity are some of the signs and messages you can convey with this gesture. Iron wires are used to make most dream catchers. Macramé dream catchers are a better choice than those who do not have any style or feel. When you come close enough to meet macramé dream catchers, they are soft and sensitive, providing a sense of warmth and gentleness. Fabrics and braids used in their development are deliberately chosen and woven together. If you add beads, feathers, and other decorative materials to your dream catcher, it will become more appealing and vibrant. You may participate in this basic yet useful craft to give your home a luxurious feel.

• Macramé Curtains

Curtains are a popular feature of many houses. There isn't a single house you step into that doesn't have a curtain or anything close in one of the rooms. Curtains are used to divide rooms in the home, from windows to doors to exits and walkways. Curtains may also be used to add a decorative element to a space. The designs and colours used to make the curtain will determine how lovely and aesthetic it will be. There are several weaves to pick from, each with a different degree of complexity. Some are thick, while others are light and have been loosened to allow light to penetrate. The macramé curtains may also be wired up to a runner so that they can be opened with ease whenever they are needed.

• Room Dividers

Macramé can be used to make room dividers, which are used to partition interior rooms. They're frequently made of loud beads. The macramé dividers are built to keep the noises produced by the rattling beads to a minimum. If you want to keep the doors closed, you should connect the dividers to the door frames to make the interior room feel more spacious and welcoming. The macramé room divider's cords are threaded with beads on strands so that they have a little weight even when disturbed, allowing them to return to their original location. This is useful for concealing exits and establishing a buffer between rooms that are close in proximity.

• Lampshade

The bulk of the old styles we have in our homes are now obsolete and unattractive. At this point, macramé lamp stands come in handy. Allowing your dusty old lampshades to be covered with macramé will turn them into something exquisite and full of life. We can effectively render them in various colours and sizes due to the ease of which the knots can be changed. You may choose how much light is permitted to pass through the lampstand. Some people choose something that lets a small amount of light in, which they do by weaving patterns that are denser and heavier. You may also make the lampstands more intricate and difficult to discern by inserting shells, beads, and tassels while maintaining the charm they produce.

• Furniture Covers

When you move into a lot of homes and businesses, you'll find the furniture is a prerequisite. They're one of the materials that you can't do without. You'll also need a macramé-designed covering to make them more appealing, even though they're made and modelled from woods of all tastes and consistency. Having them covered with macramé-made covers, whether they've really begun to look old or not, is a nice way to preserve their charm. Wait to see how your passion for the furniture is rekindled with the arrival of macramé covers, even though you find you've lost interest in getting it around. This finish transforms your worn-out and out-of-date stools and seat furniture into a thing of beauty.

• Pillows and Blankets

Pillows have surpassed mattresses as the most common sleeping material for a variety of reasons. Some for medicinal purposes, most likely due to the need to keep the head in a certain posture while sleeping. Others provide sleeping comfort and convenience. Some pillows are so well-designed that they make you feel at ease the moment you touch them. Any chair attachments can be created with macramé-style pillows that make you feel relaxed and calm when you sit on them. Blankets are useful when you have company and the air temperature decreases significantly. This decrease in temperature would necessitate the use of adequate cold-weather protection. If you want the best experience of comfort, you can make macramé your first choice when choosing fabrics to use in the development of such.

• Table Runner

Macramé table runners have a distinctive impact and style that will bring attention to your dining areas. Some dining rooms seem to be devoid of any sort of art or aesthetic appeal. Negative spaces are the term for these results. Macramé runners can be used to break up these negative spaces. When guests join your rooms, the style of table runner they see will act as an invitation to return again and again. It's a big psychological impact you're having on them. This does not only apply to home dining rooms; it also applies to bars, eateries, and fast food establishments. This will have a more tailored service for the clients. There are a lot of players vying for your customers' company. You will hold them coming back if you provide them with good service. Designing your dining area with macramé table runners is one easy way to ensure this. Flowers, candles, and certain centrepieces may be arranged on macramé runners in gardens and living rooms. This does not take up any extra eating space, so why not do it to make your dining room more relaxed and welcoming? Attach a long fringe at both ends of the table runner to take things a step further. When you go on spring vacations or hang out with friends and family, you can also enjoy these macramé table runners. They have the ability to add a bright touch and charm, believe me. Since people can see them from a closer perspective, macramé designs for table runners are more common. When the vision is a little far out, the perspective is different; because you are sitting next to it, you can quickly note the shapes and weaving lines.

• Textile Frames

You may want to use macramé frames to provide a comparison with the focal point on your frames. You should be assured that problems of confidence and compatibility can be avoided thanks to personalised designs. When we talk about frames, we're not just talking about them for the home. These frames can be found in a variety of settings, including workplaces, restaurants, rooms, and more.

Are you enjoying this book? If so, I would be really happy if you could leave a review on Amazon. It helps me to understand how I can improve the book for you. Thank You very much!

CHAPTER TWO
The Basics Of Macramé

- TERMINOLOGIES

While macramé has become quite a popular art, in some patterns there are still many words and abbreviations that people may not be aware of or may not know the meaning of.

- Adjacent: next to each other.

- Alternating: Attach a knot to one cord and then move to tie another cord to the same knot.

- ASK: Alternating knots of the square. This abbreviation is often used in macramé patterns because square knots are commonly used.

- Band: A long and smooth piece of macramé.

- Bar: A set of knots in the design that create an elevated position.

- Bight: A small folded cord portion that is forced through the knot's other sections.

- Body: You're working on the main section of the project.

- Braid: Braids are sometimes also known as plaits and are formed to loop around each other by connecting three or four cords.

- Braided cord: A type of cord consisting of several thinner pieces of cord woven together. Twisted cords tend to be more durable than twisted cords.

- Bundles: A series of cords that have been stored.

- Knot button: A tight, round decorative knot.

- BH: The button's door. Vertical lark head nodes are used to create a loop that could be used for fastening or joining parts.

- Chinese Macramé: Knotted designs from China and other countries in Asia.

- Combination knot: To create a new type of knot or design feature, use two or more knots.

- Cords: Cords is any fiber material that is used to build projects with macramé.

- Core: The cord / s running through a project's center and knotting around it. These are sometimes referred to as fillers or main strings.

- Crook: The curved part of a cord loop.

- Diagonal: A line or row of knots extending from top right to bottom (or vice versa) Diagonal knots such as half-hitch knots are often used in macramé designs.

- Diameter: The width usually in millimeters of a cord.

- DDH: Half hitch double. This concept of macramé means connecting two knots of half-hitch next to each other.

- Fillers: cords that remain at the core of a pattern and are knotted around it. Also referred to as core cords.

- Findings: objects and fastenings other than cords that can be used to construct loops, fasteners and other functional objects or decorations in macramé designs. There are examples of ear wires and clasps.

- Finishing knot: A knot tied to secure the ends of the cord and to prevent them from unravelling.

- Fringe: Cord ends lengths not knotted but left suspended.

- Knots of fusion: Another term for knots of combination.

- Gusset: A term used to design a 3D project's sides like a bag.

- Hitch: A knot commonly used to tie cords to other

items.

- Interlace: Cords are intertwined and woven together to link various areas.

- Cord knotting: the cord used in a design to tie the knots.

- LH: Knot of the head of larks.

- Loop: The circular or oval shape created by the crossing of two parts of a cord.

- Micro-Macramé: Macramé projects made using materials that are delicate or small in diameter. Micro-macramé is often defined as any macramé using cords with a diameter of less than 2 mm.

- Mount: An object that is used as part of a macramé project, such as a brace, frame or handle. For example: cords mounted on wooden handles at the beginning of a project with a macramé bag.

- Natural: Generally, this term is used to refer to cords and refers to any material made from plants, wood and other natural substances such as hemp and cotton.

- Netting: A series of knots with open spaces between them. Netting is often used to build things like bags and hangers for plants.

- OH: Knot overhand.

- Picot: Loops on the sides of a design that stand out. These are seen more often in early trends.

- Plait: Cords are plated in an alternating pattern by crossing three or more. Also referred to as a braid.

- Scallops: Knots loops created along the edges of the design of a macramé.

- Segment: Common knot, cord or design areas.

- Seniti: This term, also known as a sonnet, is a single chain of identical knots.

- Standing end: The cord end was secured on a macramé board or other surface and did not build knots.

- SK: Square knot– A common knot created by attaching two cords to one or more cords.

- Stitch: Stitch is sometimes used instead of knot in early patterns.

- Synthetic: Man-made fibers such as polypropylene and nylon.

- Vertical: from top to bottom to top.

- Vintage: A pattern, knot, or technique popular in or earlier in the early 1900s. Some vintage knots and patterns are still being used unchanged in macramé today, although others have evolved or disappeared.

- Weaving: Weaving cords means placing them under each other or over each other.

- Working cord: Another term used to knot cord. The cord with which you are currently working.

THE ESSENTIAL TOOLS AND MATERIALS YOU NEED TO HAVE

Jute, hemp, and linen, as well as other fabrics, were used mostly for nets and fabric in Macramé's practical beginnings. As sailors and traders gathered numerous types of materials from the lands to which they sailed, they aided in the building and transmission of the craft.

Quick forward to now, where we have modern technologies, materials, and, of course, the Internet, and you have access to the most beautiful array of fibres, beads, and discoveries to make just about everything you can think of.

Macramé, on the other hand, necessitates more than just thread, beads, and observations. Many of the materials you'll need to complete the tasks are likely already in your possession. You can find anything you don't have on hand easily at the favourite bead or art shop, or even the nearest hardware store in some situations.

Much of the equipment and many of the supplies mentioned would be something you already have in your workbox whether you are an avid beader or crafter. You don't have to buy anything at once because you can still improvise, but it's better to use identical materials or the equipment and resources listed for the best performance.

• Macramé Boards

When working on a macramé product, you'll need to secure it to a surface with T pins and/or masking tape. This makes playing with the cords smoother and helps keep the knots tight and balanced. Specially designed macramé boards are sold in the nearest bead or art store, as well as online stores, which work with most projects. They are normally made of fiberboard and measure 12″ x 18″ (30 cm x 46 cm). The bulk of macramé boards have a grid on the top as well as rulers on the edges. They can be discarded, but I like to keep them shrink-wrapped or locked in place because I find them to be very useful aids while I'm working. Simple macramé knots are often used as educational examples for others.

You can need to make your own macramé board if your project is too big to fit on a normal one. Choose a porous surface; you'll be able to pin your job more easily. You'll probably want to choose a surface to which you can apply, remove, and reposition tape repeatedly without causing harm. For larger projects, I've used the top of an old desk. I once built a 3' x 6' (91 cm x 183 cm) wooden board to get the job done for a long curtain. If you're going to make your own macramé board, you'll need to draw a grid on it and add rulers to the edges. If you're operating on an unusual surface, like a table or an aeroplane tray, you may want to stick a sheet of tape with dimensions written on it so you have a reference point nearby.

• Pins and Tape Pins

Your project is locked to your macramé board with pins so it doesn't jump around while you're working. They're also useful for keeping strands in place while incorporating various knot sequences and other design features into the designs.

T-pins are the most popular macramé alternative. They're a decent weight, and their shape makes it simple to insert and extract them repeatedly. Ball-end pins, which are used for weaving, may also be used, although they are not as powerful as T-pins. From using pushpins and thumbtacks because they're both too short.

Masking tape is often used to secure items to the work surface. It can be used to secure "filler cords," or cords that you tie your working cords around while tying square and twisting knots, if you're working on a more delicate surface. It's most often used to secure "filler cords," or cords that you tie your working cords around while tying square and twisting knots. (You can find more about these on the following pages.)

The blue painter's masking tape happens to be easier to strip and reposition when working than traditional masking tape. Remove duct tape, packing tape, or some other clear tape as soon as possible; they're all too sticky and can scratch the cords and surfaces, plus they're difficult to remove all over.

• Scissors

Many macramé designs are made of thin fibres that can be easily cut with a pair of fashion scissors you possibly already have. When a job is done, you may want to get a pair of tiny sewing trimming scissors to trim the excess length. They'll allow you to get up close and personal with any knot you want to break.

Hide and string suede and leather are included in many of the projects in this book. Those would require the use of a more efficient pair of scissors. There are beautiful economical scissors from the leather shop that have become my favourite perfect all-around scissors. They can accommodate the skins, but they're small enough to cut ends around knots and are ideal for almost anything else. If you're going to be working with these products extensively, investing in a good pair of scissors is a good idea.

• Adhesives

To secure the final knot in most macramé designs, adhesive is used (s). The type of adhesive to use would be determined by the materials used. White glue works well for waxed linen, hemp, cotton, silk, and other fabrics. Rubber cement or touch cement are suitable for leather and suede. E-6000 and epoxy are non-porous adhesives that are used to glue non-porous items together, such as wire and labradorite crystals, which are used with the heart belt's buckle. Both of these adhesives require good ventilation when in operation, which should be strictly followed by all warning labels.

• Cords

You'll actually be able to macramé with it if you can tie a knot. Two of the most common fibre varieties for working with are waxed linen and waxed hemp. They are available in a number of colours and thicknesses. The wax covering on such cords makes it exceedingly convenient to tie a knot. Your knots and knot patterns will be well represented as a result. Bead and design stores sell these cords, and you can quickly find them online.

Rattail, a satin cord that comes in a rainbow of colours and at least three different thicknesses, is another common macramé material. Rattail was common in the 1970s and has never gone out of style among artisans who like to incorporate Chinese or Celtic knots into their work. It can be slick, and well-knotted rattail knots can unravel if not secured. However, the end product is so lovely that it's well worth the effort. Chain of polypropylene or polyolefin. It's used to make rope for boating, travel, and any other activity that requires a powerful, durable, and waterproof material. It's also suitable for purses, hammocks, and the leash and collar project. Although the colour palette is small, the realistic properties make it a feasible alternative for many pursuits. This is available at the local hardware store.

Macramé fabrics such as leather and lace suede are awesome. There are a variety of lace weights to choose from. Look for laces that are smoother and more supple, rather than stiffer ones that might be difficult to tie. When deciding which method of hiding to use, think about the form and intent of your project. Is it a major win? Is he a jerk? Is it appropriate for the material to be rugged and ready to crack, or will it be handled with more care? I've used a thin, lightweight suede for tiny pockets, a beaded curtain, and even a chain, but a larger bag would need a heavier, more sturdy lace, which I've learned through experience. Ultra-Suede is a cloth and suede substitute. Ultra-suede is a stain-resistant synthetic cloth that has a suede-like texture that is machine washable. It's used in a variety of shades as well as a few different thicknesses. Numerous styles, shapes, and colours of leather, suede, and ultra-suede are available in the nearest bead, craft, or leather store, as well as online.

Cotton and wool yarns are used in a scarf, a belt, and even a halter top in this book's accessories. There are so many lovely yarns out there, and I must admit that I've always been envious of knitters and their infinite possibilities! I, on the other hand, have no inclination to crochet. However, I'm interested in the wool. When you're at the yarn shop, play around with your choices. Bamboo thread, cashmere, alpaca, angora, and other natural fabrics, as well as cotton and wool blends, come in a variety of textures. The chunky, variegated yarns are my favourites (like the one I used for the scarf). Allow yourself to be pampered with luscious, hand-tinted fibres.

• Choosing cords

If you've mastered a method, try experimenting with various materials and see what you can come up with. When working with a soft cord like satin rattail or embroidery cottons, knots can lose definition, but when using a stiffer cord like Superlon™, waxcotton, or round leather thong, the outline can be even more distinct. Think how you want the finished item to look before you begin, and select your cordor thread accordingly. Remember all each of these cords comes in a variety of thicknesses and can be used individually or in various bundles.

• Cord guide

This cord sample board displays some of the cords that are appropriate for macramé at a glance, as well as the variety of thicknesses available in the various cords.

• Satin cord (rattail)

This silky cord has a high sheen and is available in a range of thicknesses: bugtail is 1mm thick, mousetail 1.5mm thick, and rattail is 2mm thick, however, in practice all tend to be called rattail now. The cord is quite soft so it doesn't support the shape of knots very well and it isn't very hard-wearing.

• Chinese knotting cord

When employed, this nylon braided cord retains its circular form. The finer strings, which are currently available in 0.4–3mm, are more common for macramé. Look online for the most varied colour palettes, but bear in mind that the colour selection for thicker cords can be minimal relative to finer cords.

• Wax cotton cord

Wax cotton cord may be used in a variety of ways. Look for 3mm thread, which is thicker and keeps its form better, making it ideal for individual knots and knotted braids. Wax cotton that is thinner and easier to thread with beads is suitable for macramé. They come in a variety of natural tones and colours, all of which are in line with emerging fashion trends.

- Superlon™

SuperlonTM (also known as S-lonTM) is a high-strength twisted nylon string that was first used for upholstery. It comes in two widths: 0.5mm and 0.9mm, and both are sufficient for micro macramé and other knotting techniques that involve a fine braid or finish. These cords are suitable for inserting beads into knotting and can be combined with thicker cords for a different feel. Both sizes come in a variety of neutrals and pretty contemporary hues.

- Paracord

This thick cord is usually available in two thicknesses: paracord 550 (4mm) has seven strands down the middle, while paracord 450 (2mm) has four. Because of its bulk, paracord is famous for men's jewellery. It's ideal for making bracelets and other accessories from single knots. The cord comes in a variety of strong light and dark colours, as well as a variety of multicoloured designs.

- Leather thong

Since it is a firm thread, a round leather thong makes a nice distinct knot. It comes with a variety of thicknesses ranging from 0.5mm to 6mm. Thinner cords are better for binding knots, and thicker cords are better for using as a core for tying knots throughout. Leather thongs are sold in a variety of colours and natural shades. The various thicknesses of snakeskin influence strings, as well as pearlescent finishes in pale pastels, are especially appealing.

• Faux suede

This flat microfibre cord has the appearance of real leather suede, but it is much more pliable and giving knots a slightly different look. It's typically 3mm thick and comes in a variety of colours.

• Embroidery threads

Macramé can be done with stranded cotton and cotton perlé, which are also readily available threads. Embroidery threads are delicate and won't maintain a knot's form as well as stiffer cords, but they look fine when paired. Since the colour spectrum is much wider than that of other strings, exclusive colour combinations are possible. While most embroidery threads are matte, metallic embroidery threads will add a bit of glitz.

• Findings

Findings are all the small pieces, mostly made of metal, that go into making and finishing jewellery and other accessories. Many of the results are used to cover the raw ends of strings, so choosing the right size and form is crucial. Hold a variety of results in your workbox so you can build and complete a variety of tasks.

• Finishing ends

The ends of knotted strings are done with findings. Year after year, more and more styles are produced, with the majority of them available in a variety of metallic finishes. Match the internal lengths of the finishing ends to the rope or braid for the optimal performance. Often finishing ends have a fastening, but this isn't always the case.

• Cord ends

Some models have lugs that you clamp over the string with pliers, while others are tubular and are sealed either with glue or with an integral crimpring.

• Spring ends

This are one of the more traditional styles of finding, and they can be cylindrical or cone-shaped. Squeeze just the end ring with pliers to protect the cord or braid within the wire coil.

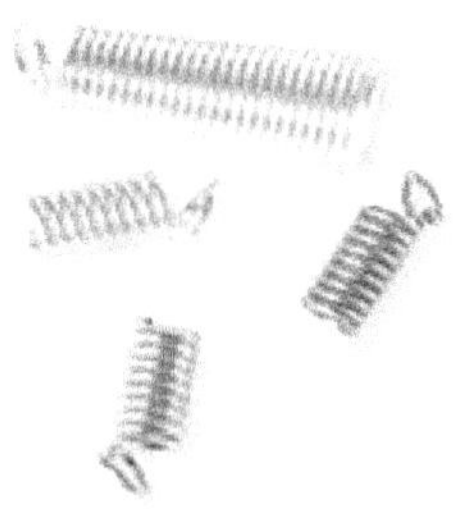

• End cones

These cone or bell-shaped findings may be completed with a hole or a circle at the end. Using jewellery glue to lock the braid into both types for the best results.

• End caps

End caps are cylindrical, square, or rectangular versions of end cones that have a hole in the top or are ready-finished with a ring or circle. Using jewellery glue to lock the braid into both types for the best results.

• Ribbon crimps

These are intended to cover the raw end of ribbon, but they may also be used to finish flat braids or rope, as the name implies. Close the ribbon crimp over the braid with nylon-jaw pliers to save it from being hurt.

• Jewellery fastenings

Findings are used to complete jewellery such as necklaces, bracelets, earrings, and rings in a number of ways. I've selected a few models of fastenings that work well for macramé. End caps with a magnetic fastening are used in some of the fastenings; otherwise, choose a design that suits the end cap and complements the braid in colour and weight.

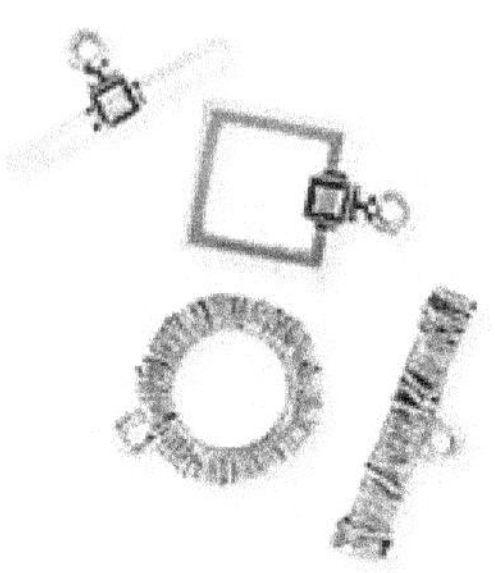

- Toggle fastening

A T-bar and a ring make up this two-part fastening; turn the T-bar on its side to slot into or out of the ring. As a design feature, go with a more decorative look.

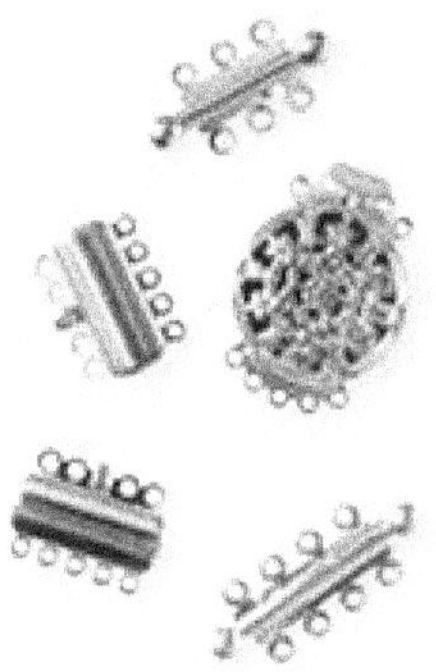

- Magnetic fastenings

A solid magnet is built into the design of these neat fastenings. They're ideal for adding a finishing touch to necklaces and bracelets.

• Trigger clasp

This low-cost clasp has a spring closure which can be used to complete both bracelets and necklaces. The lobster claw and bolt ring are two models that are available.

• Multi-strand clasps

This come in a variety of designs. The slider fastening is perfect for macramé and other cuff-style bracelets, and the box design is appropriate for necklaces. To suit the project, determine the number of rings on each hand.

• Plastic clasps

These plastic clasps have a bar end to tie the cords to, making them ideal for knotting techniques like macramé. The clasps are available in a number of sizes and vibrant colours.

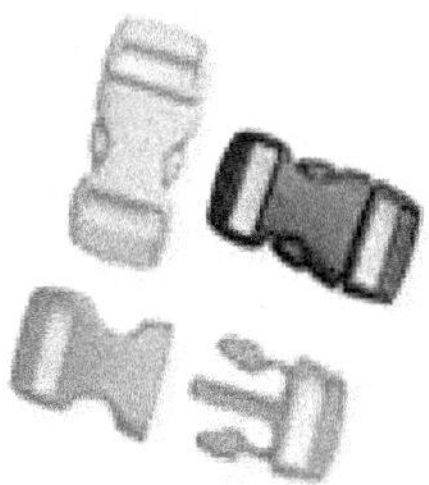

• Beads

Beads may be inserted into any macramé technique in a number of ways, either during the knotting process or afterward.

• Choosing beads

Beads come in a variety of colours, finishes, heights, and

forms, but the size of the hole is critical for knotting so the beads must be quickly strung onto the string. When you go bead shopping, it's a smart idea to bring a sample of cord with you.

• Seed beads

This is a catch-all word for tiny glass beads used especially for bead stitching and stringing. The most common sizes for basic seed beads (rocailles) are 15 to 3 (1–5.5mm), with 15 (1mm) being the smallest; cylinder-shaped beads, also known as delicas or magnificas, have wider holes, and the double delicas can be strung on 1mm thread. Look for various shapes like papillon (or peanut) beads and magatamas, as well as odd textures like triangle, hex, or charlotte beads (drop beads).

• Large beads

From plain wood beads to beautiful pearls and crystals, there are several different beads that can be used in knotting techniques, and the choice is yours. Some beads, such as the Swarovski Mini-bead range, have remarkably wide holes, allowing even the 6mm beads to fit into 1mm cord. Beads in the Pandora style have wide holes and can fit over 6mm thread.

• Beads for focal points

These extra-large beads are often used as a focal point in jewellery designs. To work macramé, use a bail to hang pendant beads or tie cords to big ring beads. Big beads may also be strung between two lengths of macramé that have been completed with end caps.

• Wire

The essence of metal is that it should not bend repeatedly. It's weak, and bending it repeatedly allows it to become brittle and work-hardened. It will eventually break if you repeatedly bend it back and forth. Heavier wire often resists bending without a great deal of work. The bulk of metal macramé is manufactured of thinner gauge wire and is simpler to deal with. It will still stiffen when it is running, but the less you bend it, the better.

If you've never worked with wire before, you may want to start with a less expensive metal wire to get a feel for it. There are a variety of wire varieties to pick from, including brass, bronze, and art wire, all of which are available in a variety of colours. The majority of these coils, also known as gauges, come in a variety of thicknesses. The lower the gauge number, the more difficult it is to bend the wire due to its thickness.

CHAPTER THREE

Macramé Techniques And Basics

It's time to get started with the strategies now that you know what you'll need. This segment of the book will take you through all of the simple knots and teach you how to adapt them to various macramé techniques. If you've perfected these, you'll be able to make a range of lovely jewellery for yourself and your loved ones.

KNOTTING BASICS

If you are familiar with the words widely used, you can find that the directions for constructing knots are far simpler to obey. Before beginning some macramé techniques, it is also a good practise to familiarise yourself with the simple knots.

Knotting Terms

Take a few moments to become familiar with the knotting terminology that are commonly used in step-by-step directions, the bulk of which are outlined below.

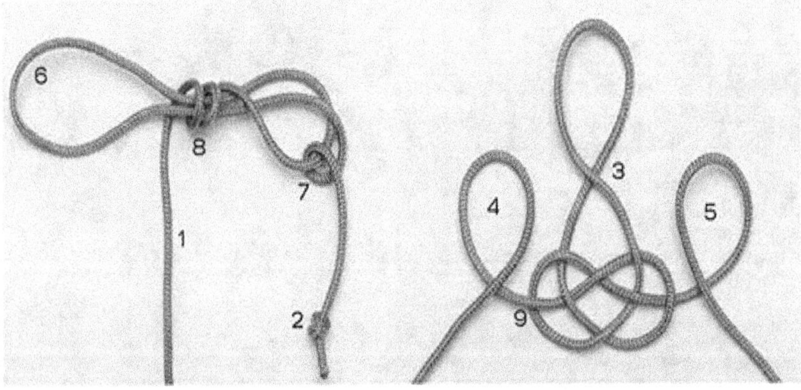

Working end (1) The end of the cord that you are using to tie the knot.

Starting end (2) The opposite end to the working end – if you begin in the middle of a cord both ends are working ends.

Cross point (3) Where one cord crosses over the other. An overhand cross point is when the working end is on top, and when the working end is underneath it is an underhand cross point.

Clockwise loop (4) Sometimes referred to as an overhand loop, this is where the working end goes around clockwise and over itself again. Sometimes referred to as an underhand loop, this is where the working end goes around anticlockwise and over itself again.

U-shaped bend (6) Also known as a bight, this is often made as a way to weave cord through the knot.

Circled (7) The cord passes around one or more strands in the knot.

Coiled (8) The cord wraps around one or more strands several times.

Weave (9) To go over and under successive cords in a knot with a working end or U-shaped bend.

Firm up Tighten the knot until the cords are secure, but not so tight that the knot is distorted.

Core cord This is a stationary cord inside other threads and cords. In macramé the core cords can become working cords and vice versa.

Base cord This cord often forms the basic shape of a necklace or can be substituted for a finding, such as a solid ring, fastening or bar. The working cords are usually attached to the base cord with lark's head knots.

Tying Basic Knots

Since these simple knots are used too often, learn them by heart.

• Reef (square) knot

This is used to connect two cord ends of equal thickness, and it can be loosened by pulling one end back over the knot if necessary. In macramé, it is the foundation for the square knot.

To pull the cord up into the loop on the left, pass the left cord over the right and tuck under, then pass the right cord over the left and under.

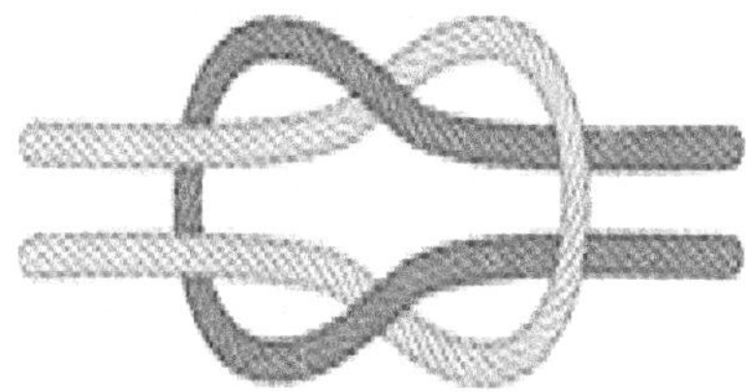

• Overhand knot

This simple knot can be tied as a stopper or a reminder of the beginning end of a rope, or it can be used to detach or bind beads, or it can be used to create a simple sliding fastening. Create a clockwise loop over the thumb and pull the operating thread up through the loop.

• Slip knot

The slip knot is the foundation of many knotted braids because it allows the working end to be adjusted. Make an anticlockwise loop and keep the rope in your left hand at the cross point (at the bottom). Bring the working cord behind the rope and bend it in a U shape. Pull the working end to change the loop size and the short starting end to firm up the knot.

• Lark's head

This knot is the most widely used knot for beginning macramé designs, and it is used to tie one cord to another, as well as to attach a cord to a bar or a ring, as seen here.

Fold one rope in half and weave the string from front to back around the ring. Pull up to tighten the circle by passing the tails into it. To make a reverse lark's head knot, pass the rope through the ring from the backside and finish the knot by moving the tails through the loop once more.

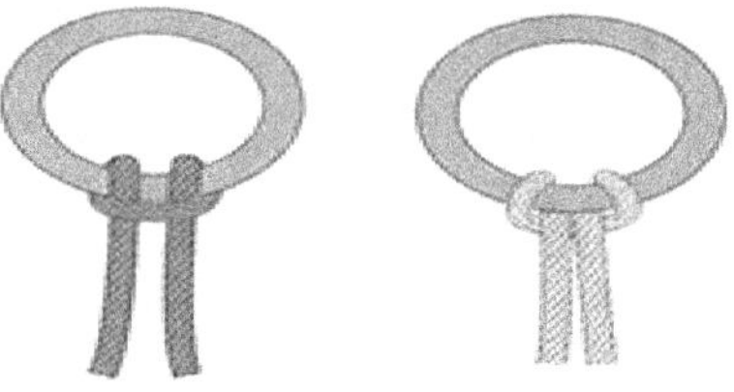

• Half-hitch

One of the most basic macramé knots, which can be worked over another cord or a ring or bar, as seen here. It's often used in pairs to keep finer cords or threads in place.

To make a half-hitch, take one cord and slip the working end under the other cord and behind the starting end. For added protection, make a second loop in the same direction, moving the working end through the loop between the two half-hitches.

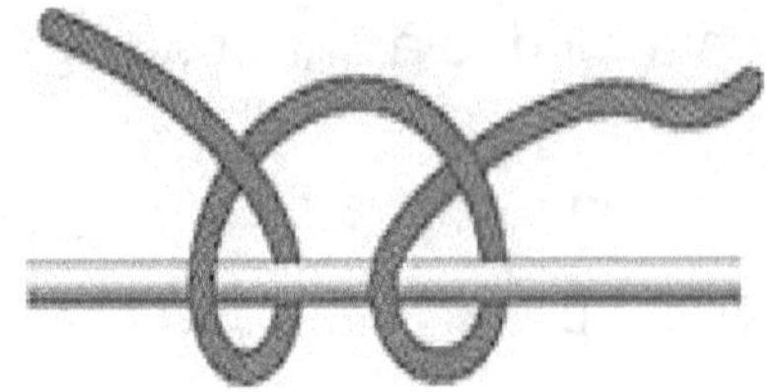

• Using Basic Knots

And the simplest knots can be used to create stunning jewellery. Overhand knots can be used to detach or connect beads, reef knots can be used to make a fast and simple bracelet, and there are several other ideas for making the most of common knots in this section.

• Overhand knots

The overhand knot looks fantastic when tucked into a rustic leather cord; it can be used to detach beads, connect charms, or even act as a basic slipping fastener.

• Use overhand knots to secure a bead to a stretch of string or to space beads along the leather's length. Choose a cord that is appropriate for the size of the bead hole.

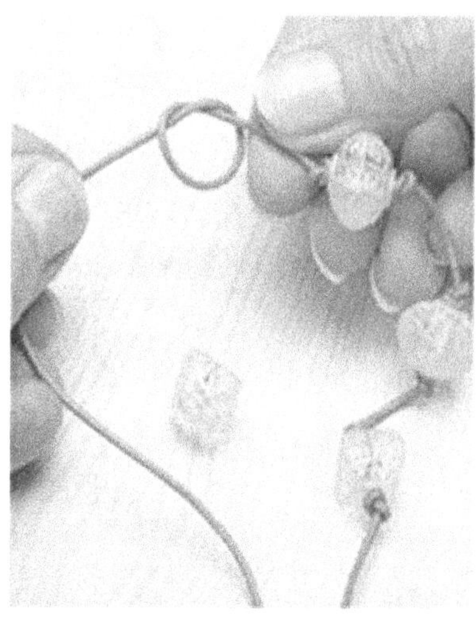

• When working with two or more strands of cord, one of them should be thinner in order to slip through small-hole beads before binding the strands together with an overhand knot.

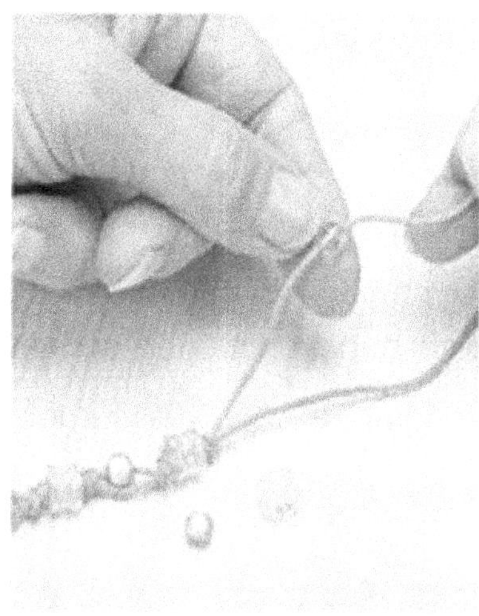

• Tie a hop ring charm or chain to the length of the rope with an overhand knot. To save the chain from bending, tie the knot by ties on the same side of the chain.

• Loop two lengths of cord through a washer-style bead or button in opposite directions, then secure with an overhand knot on either side.

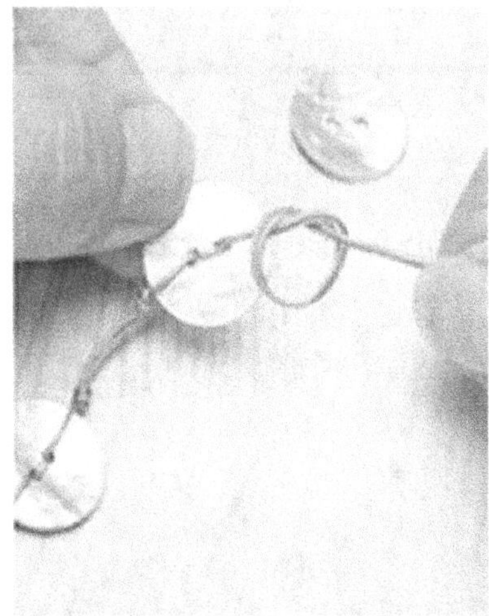

• To make a basic beaded tassel, tie a bundle of cords together with an overhand knot, then connect a bead to each strand and secure it with an overhand knot above and below the knot.

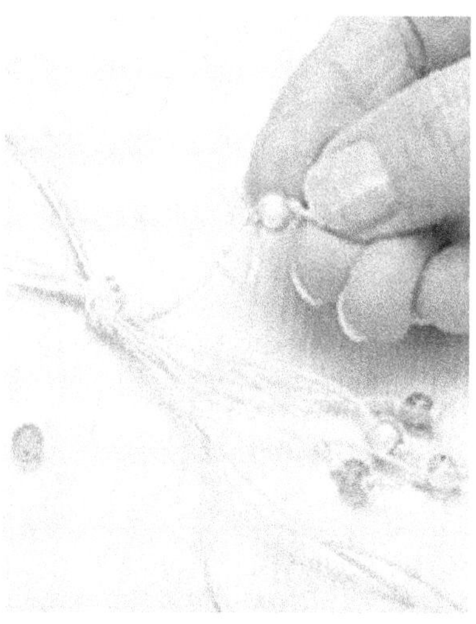

• Lay two cords ends in opposite directions for a slipping fastening, and at either end, tie an overhand knot over the other cord to firm it up. To open, pull the tails open, and to close, pull the key cord.

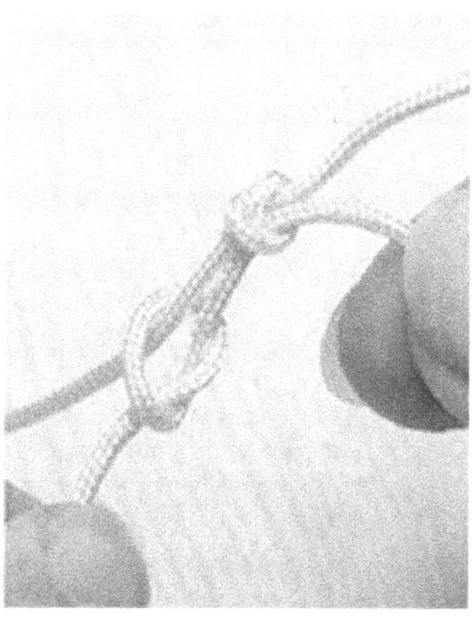

• Reef knot

Reef knots can be used to turn cord that is too dense to tie complicated knots into a simple and easy shape, suitable for making a pretty bracelet.

1. Tie a reef knot with two 25cm (10in) lengths of 6mm thread. Adjust the knot until all of the ends are the same length, then softly tug to firm it up.

2. Check the length of the cuff to allow for the fastening, trim the rope ends, and then use hard jewellery glue to tie both cords at either end to the fastening.

• Lark's head knot

This is one of the most useful knots for making jewellery and accessories, and it's always forgotten. Lark's head knots may be used to create attractive jewellery patterns in single or multiples.

• Make a slide fastening by tying lark's head knots around the rings, ready to work a large panel of macramé into a cuff bracelet.

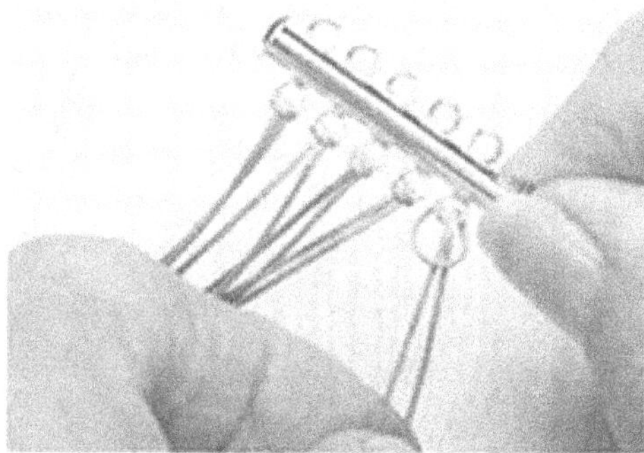

• Tie a rope to a sturdy ring with the lark's head knot to

create an apendant that can be further embellished with hop rings and beadcharms.

72

• Make a simple bracelet by tying a lark's head knot on either side of a ring or other design, then locking the ends in a fastening.

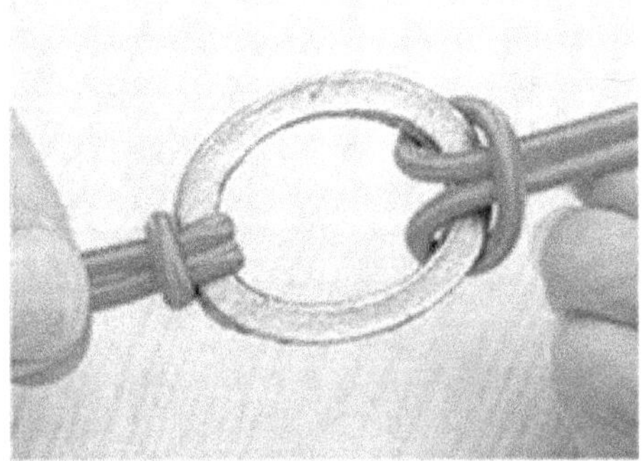

• Multiple lark's head knots

Doing the knots one by one requires a slightly different strategy, since you would weave one tail around the central cord in order for it to take the right direction for a lark's head knot.

• Single core technique

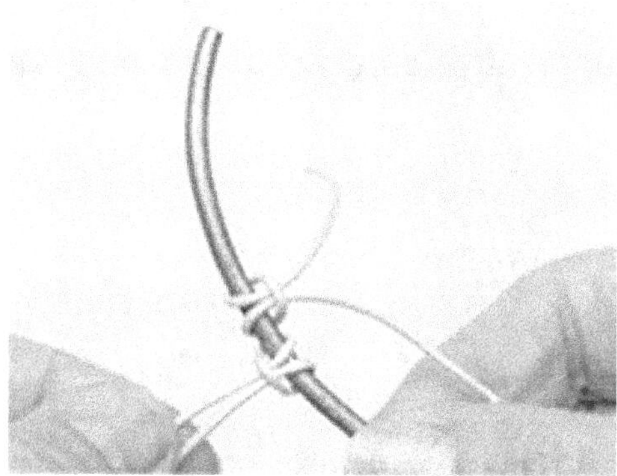

1. Clip a thin cord to one end of a thicker corecord with a lark's head knot; strap on a second length of thin cord with a lark's head knot facing the opposite way.

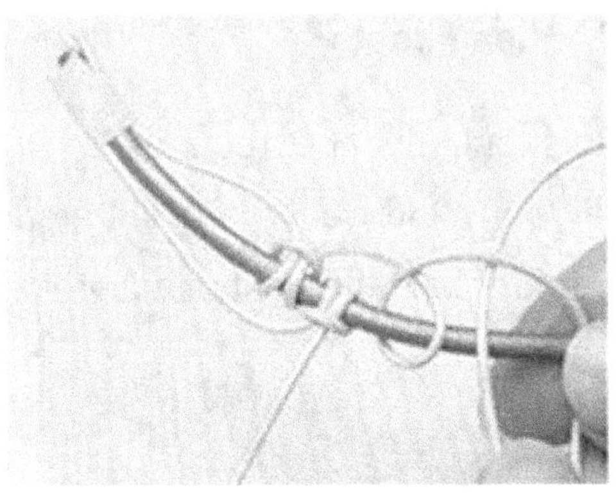

2. Work a half-hitch over the central cord with the first working end. To make a third lark's head knot, pass the working end under the core cord and back up through the loop.

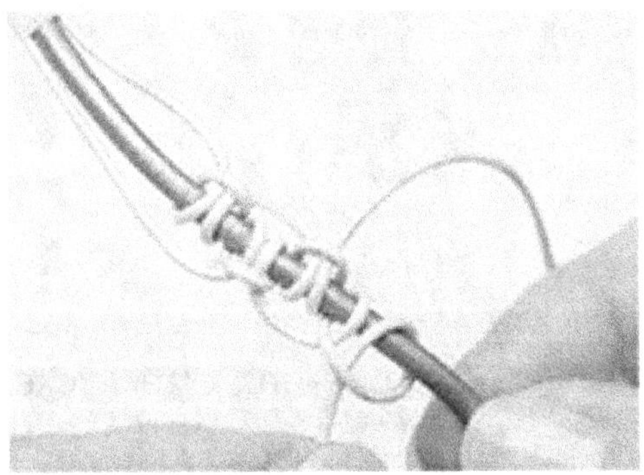

3. Work one lark's head knot at a time with alternate cords as you move from side to side. Beads may be attached to the wide loops on either foot.

- **Double core technique**

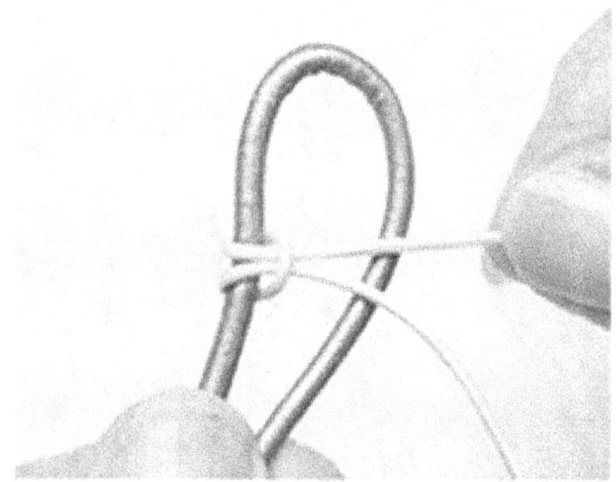

1. Tie a lark's head knot in the centre of a 40cm (16in) length of thick leather cord for a bracelet length. Take the top working chord of the lark's head knot over and across the other half of the main cord and bend it in half.

2. As in Single Core Procedure, step 2, make a second lark's head knot on the right-hand side of the rope, and then move the right-hand working chord diagonally around and over the left-hand core cord. Make a knot in the shape of a lark's head. Cross and over the right-hand core cord with the left-hand working cable. Make a new lark's head tie.

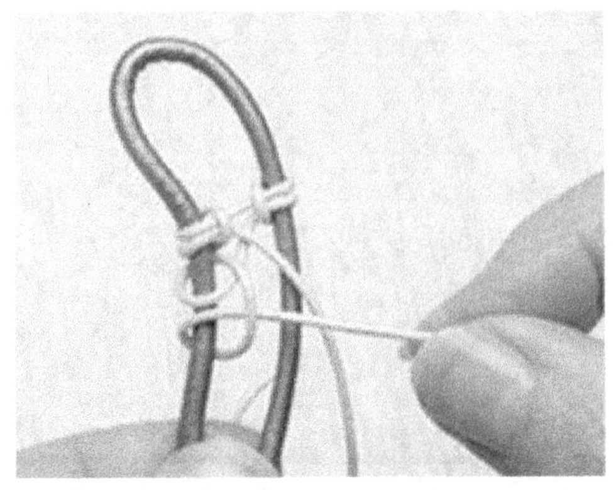

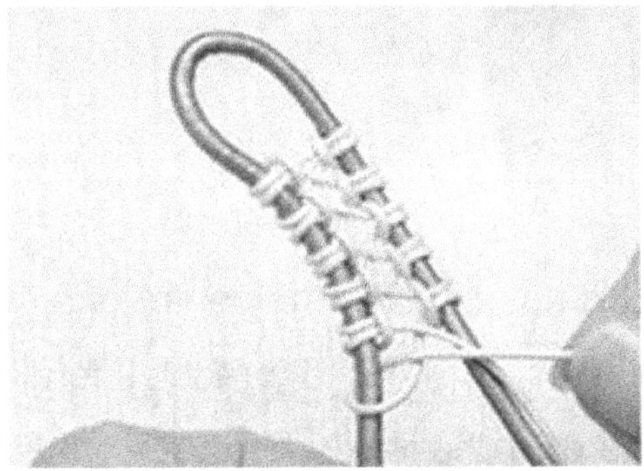

3. Continue the criss-cross lark's head knot pattern all the way down the core cords. To fit a button or click, you should change the size of the top circle.

MACRAMÉ BASICS

Macramé is said to have evolved as a way to tie or create decorative fringing on rugs or woven blankets. It is one of the most versatile knotting techniques because although there are only three basic knots, these can be used singly or in unison to create a wide range of braids, flat panels or tubular structures.

Unlike other knotted braids that are usually worked in the hand, macramé is often secured to the work surface with pins or a spring clip. The square and half-knot worked with three or four cords are easy to learn, then you can move on to multi-strand techniques and different ways to use the half-hitch.

• Estimating cord lengths

If you're switching the core and working cords around, finding out the length of cord for working macramé can be complicated, but as a general rule, the core cords should be the length of the finished piece plus 15cm (6in) at each end for finishing. Working cords can be three or four times the finished length.

• Working macramé

Working on a cork pin board or a sheet of foam core allows you to protect the cords with short map pins.

• Beginning with a loop

1. Fold a cord in half and tie it around a map pin. At the bottom of the board, use a spring clip to connect the ends. Tie an overhand knot in the middle of the working chord with a second length of cord tucked beneath the core cords.

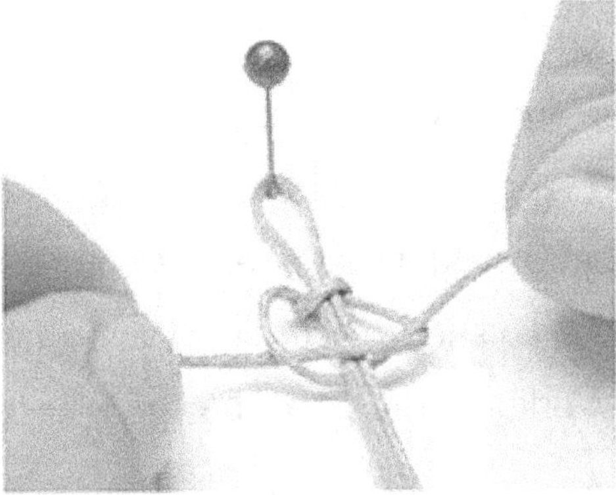

2. To make a neater finish on the front side, undo the overhand knot and begin tying the first macramé knot.

• Macramé knots

The half knot, square knot, and half-hitch are three basic knots used in macramé that can be used in various configurations to produce a range of effects and designs. This section demonstrates how to tie the two flat knots – the half-hitch and square knot; for the half-hitch, a separate method is used.

• Half Knot

This is a half-reef (square) knot (see Knotting Basics: Tying Basic Knots) that is repeated in the same direction to allow the cords to twist naturally. It can be worked over one, three, or more core cords, as seen here.

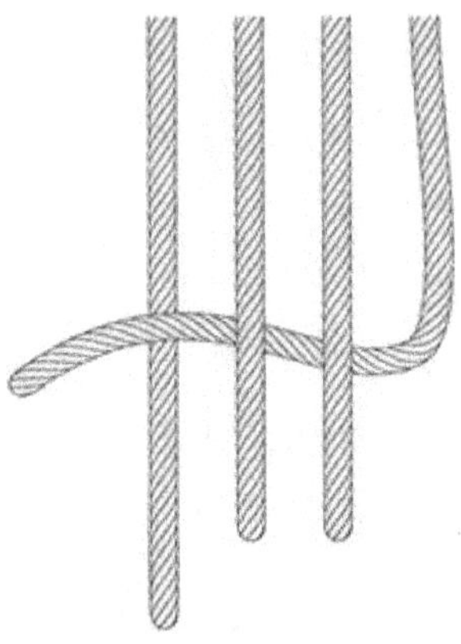

1. Cut cords according to the instructions in Estimating Cord Lengths and lay them side by side with the two shorter (core) cords in the centre. Under the central cords and over the left-hand cable, pass the right-hand cord.

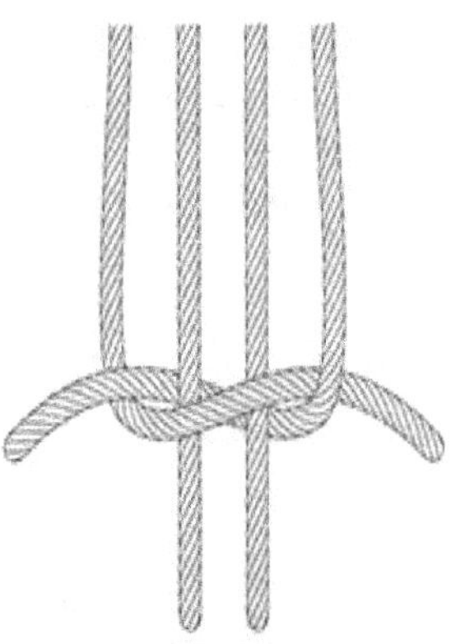

2. Cross the left-hand cord over the central cords and down into the right-hand loop. Pull the strings together to secure the knot. Repeat from * until the spiral is the length required.

- **SQUARE KNOT**

The basic technique can easily be used to build larger panels (see Multistrand Macramé: Alternating Square Knots). This flat knot is basically a reef (square) knot that is usually worked over two core cords.

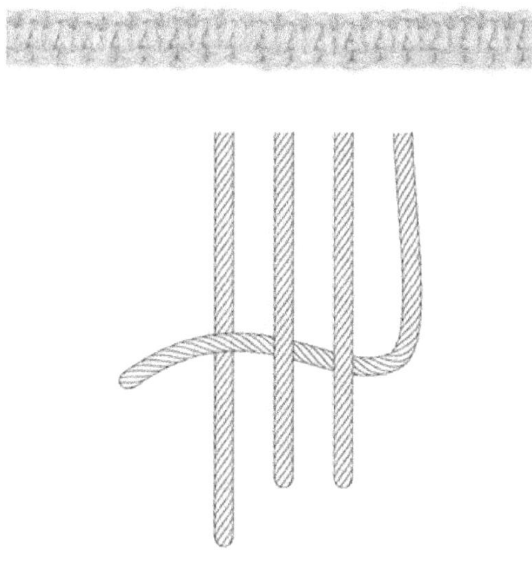

1. Arrange the cords side by side so that the two shorter (core) cords are in the middle. * Work a half knot passing the right-hand cord under the core cords and over the left-hand cord. Take the left-hand cord over the core cords and pass it down through the loop on the right.

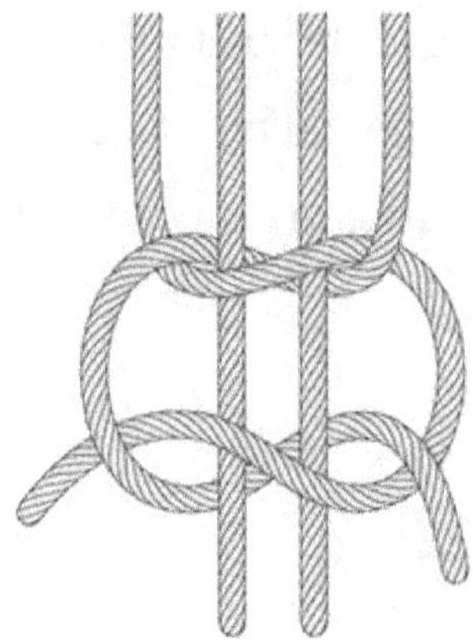

2. Reverse the process, passing the left-hand cord under the core cords and over the right-hand cord. Then take the right-hand cord and pass it down through the loop on the left. Repeat from *.

- SQUARE KNOT VARIATIONS

The square knot is a popular knot for making macramé bracelets and other para-cord accessories, and the flat knot braid that results is known as a Solomon bar. You can make a lot of interesting combinations by experimenting with various ways to manipulate the simple square knot.

• Crossed Cords

To produce a cross stitch effect, apply a contrast cord colour to the simple square knot cords and reverse with a running stitch pattern.

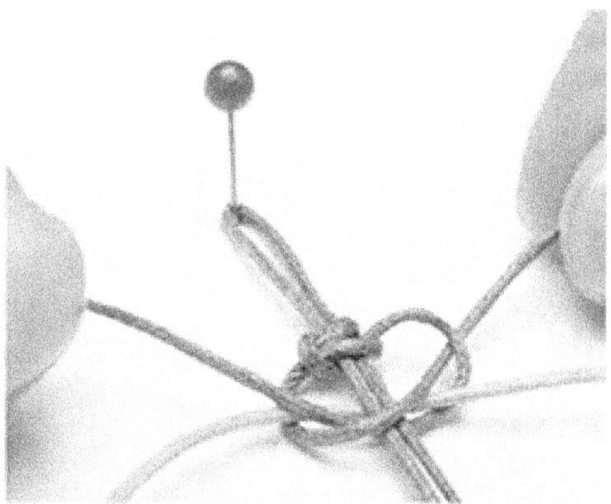

1. Start with an overhand knot and work one square knot (see Macramé Basics: Macramé Knots); before you firm up the knot, feed the ends of a contrast cord colour through the square knot under the core cords.

2. Cross the right-hand contrast cord over the left and drop the tails either side of the core cords.

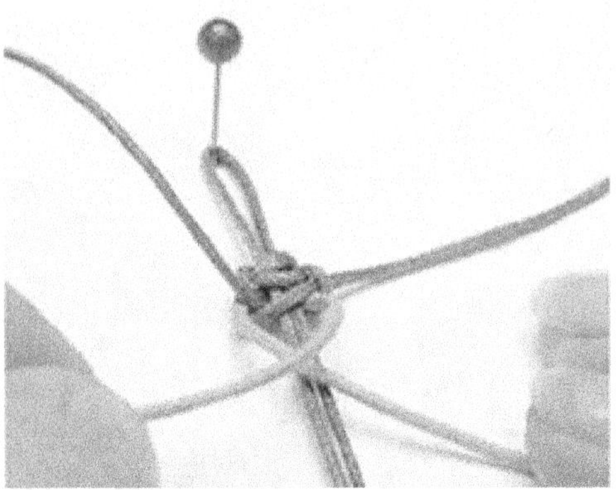

1. Work the first half of the next square knot: left-hand cord under the core cords and over the right-hand cord right-hand cord over the core cords and down through the loop on the left.

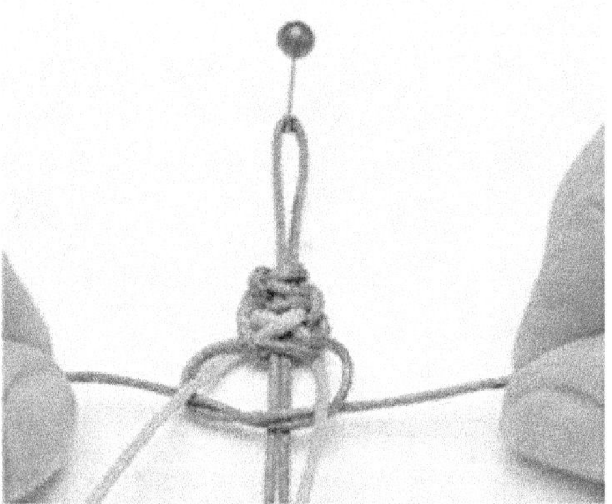

2. Lift the contrast cords up above the knots. Work the second half of the square knot, taking the right-hand cord under the contrast cords but over the core cords and the left-hand cord. Take the left-hand cord under the contrast cords but over the core cords and down through the right loop.

3. Repeat steps 2–4 continuing the pattern of crosses.
    You can cross the right cord over the left each time,
    or alternate for a different effect.

To create a running stitch pattern on both sides of the braid,
keep the contrast cords running down each side of the braid
rather than creating a cross at step 2.

• MULTI-STRAND MACRAMÉ

You can work macramé with many more cords than the basic four, to create wider bands for fringing, a belt or a cuff bracelet. Multi-strand macramé can even be worked in the round to make items such as bags or plant holders. With more than four cords, however, you do need to plan ahead, working out the design, the number of cords required, and how to secure them to start.

• Alternating square knots

Although you can work a square knot over a single cord (three cords in total), for alternating square knots it is better to work with multiples of four base cords.

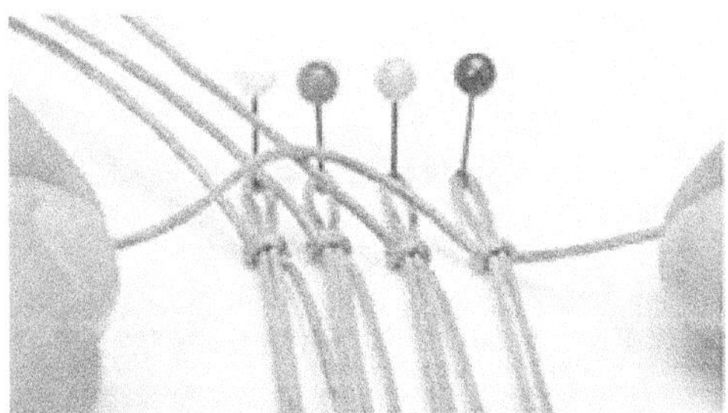

1. Ready the macramé cords by pinning the doubled-over cords to a board. For each pair of cords, tie a second cord with an overhand knot and rotate for a neater finish (see Macramé Basics: Working Macramé/Beginning with a Loop).

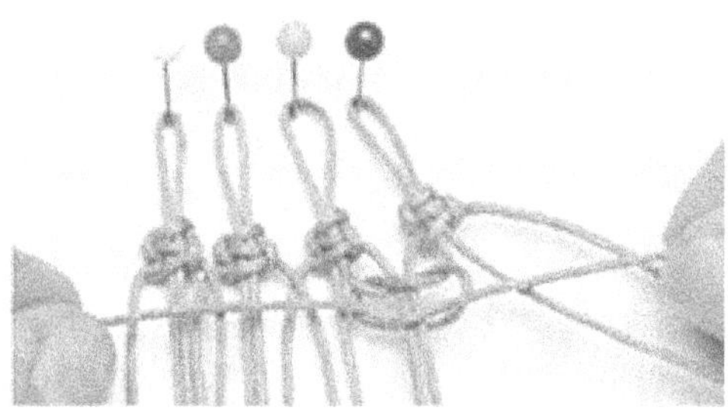

2. Tie a square knot with the first four cords (see Macramé Basics: Macramé Knots), then a square knot with the next four cords. Work your way through the cords, tying a square knot on each group of four cords until the row is complete. Tighten the knots so they don't come loose.

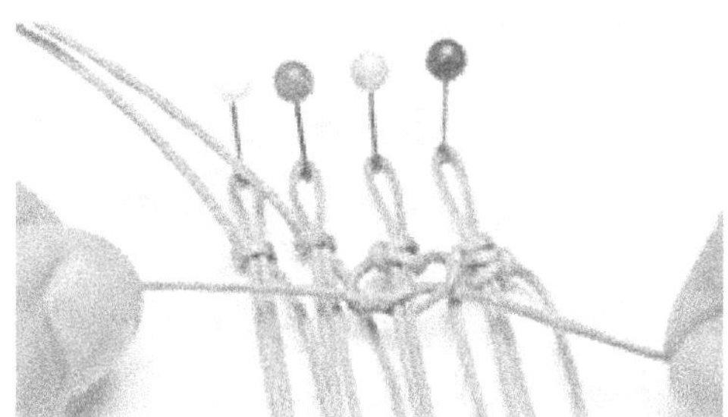

3. The operating cords from the previous row will become the central cords of the next row, and vice versa. Take the first two cords on the right-hand side and separate them. Function a square knot between the next four cords.

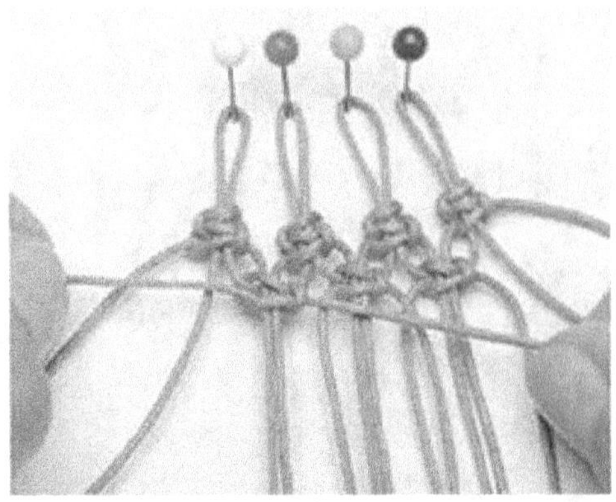

4. Work your way through the cords, tying a square knot on each set of four cords before you meet the left-hand side's final two cords.

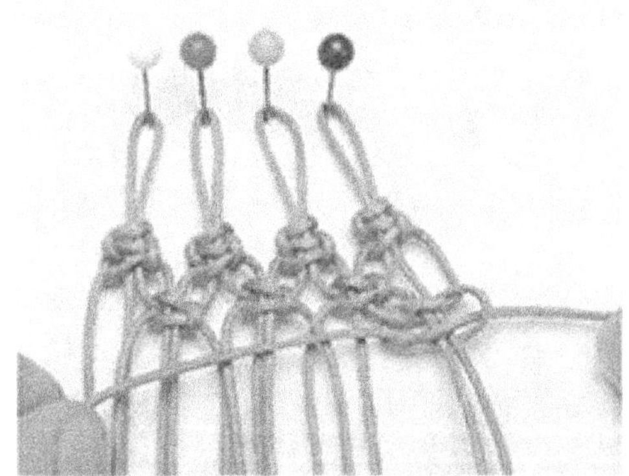

5. Carry the two extra cords down to the next row. Work the next row the same way as the previous, from right to left, tying a square knot on the first four cords and every four cords around the row.

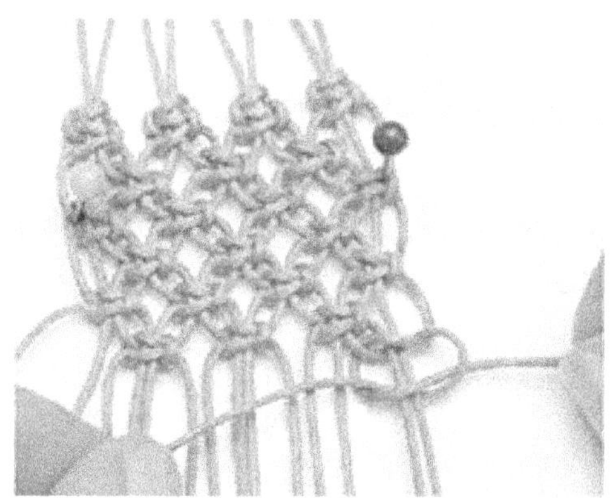

6. To create the macramé panel, keep repeating the two-row tying sequence. Try to tie knots at the same distance each time for an even panel, and use pins to secure the panel while you work down.

• Setting up a system to deal with different cords. Start working with your cords by looping them or connecting them to a fastening, buckle, or other fitting (see Macramé Basics: Working Macramé). Working on a cork pin board or foam core has the advantage of allowing you to space your knots as you go and secure cords at an angle for a more accurate piece of knotting.

• Straight half-hitch rib

Half-hitches are normally employed in pairs as a double half-hitch over one of the side cords to form a thick horizontal rib, as seen.

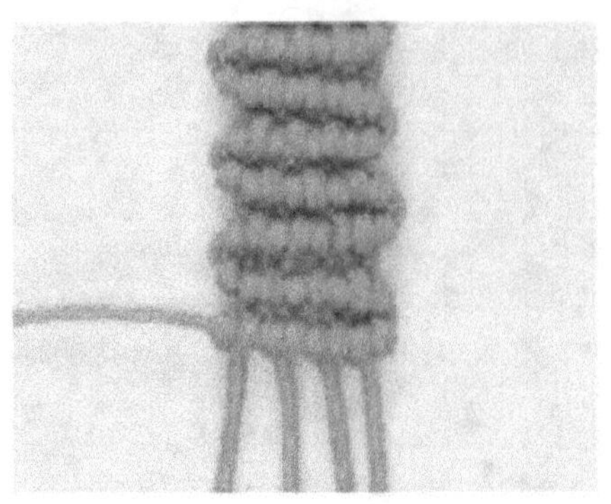

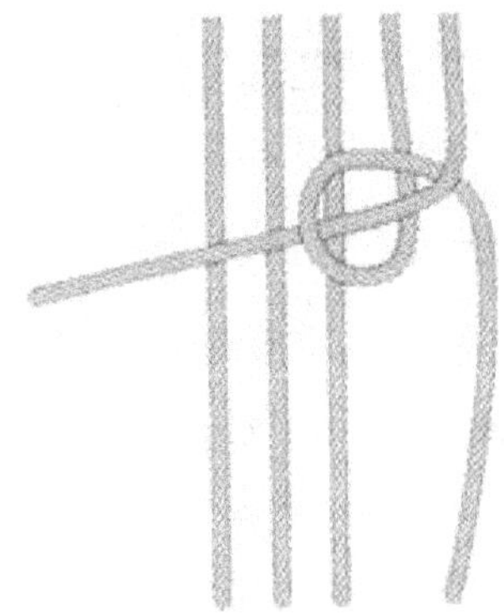

1. Position one of the outer cords horizontally over the other cords. Bring the current outer vertical cord to the right-hand line, over the horizontal cord and back under it.

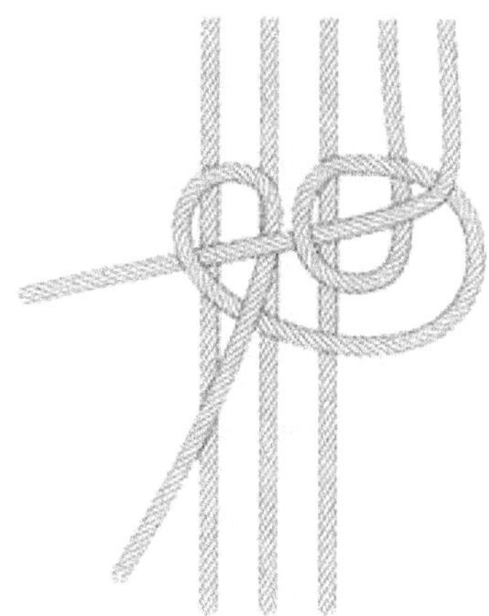

3. Take the same cord out to the right-hand side through the coil, this time over the horizontal cord. To make a dense rib, repeat the two knots on each of the vertical cords in turn. Bring the inner cord back over the vertical cords and repeat the procedure in the opposite direction as you reach the end.

✓ Angled-edge half-hitch rib

Half-hitches are often used to make panels with shaped sides. To work straight half-hitch, one side cord is taken back and forwards, but if you use successive cords on a particular side the edge will be angled instead.

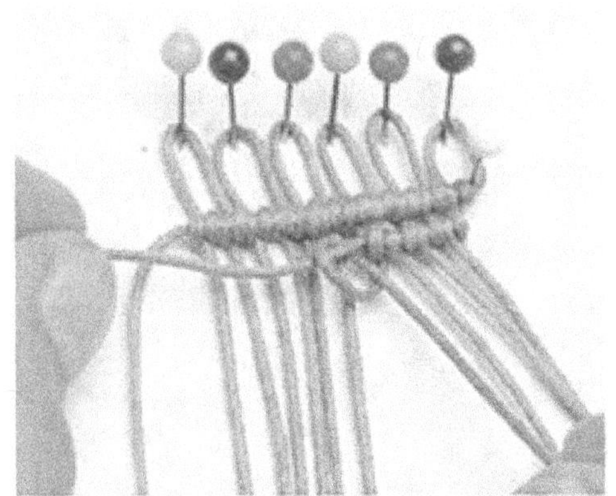

1. Pin the right-hand cord across the other vertical cords. Work one row of half-hitch rib across this core cord, tying double half-hitches with each vertical cord. Pin the next right-hand cord across under the rib. Work a row of half-hitch rib over the new core cord finishing with a double half-hitch over the previous core cord on the left-hand side.

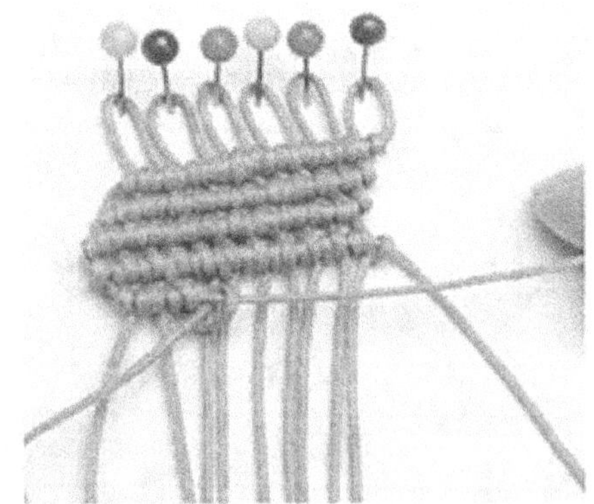

2. Pin the next right-hand cord across under the rib and work another row of half-hitches – already the panel has begun to shape diagonally. Do remember to work half-hitches over the previous core cord at the end of each row.

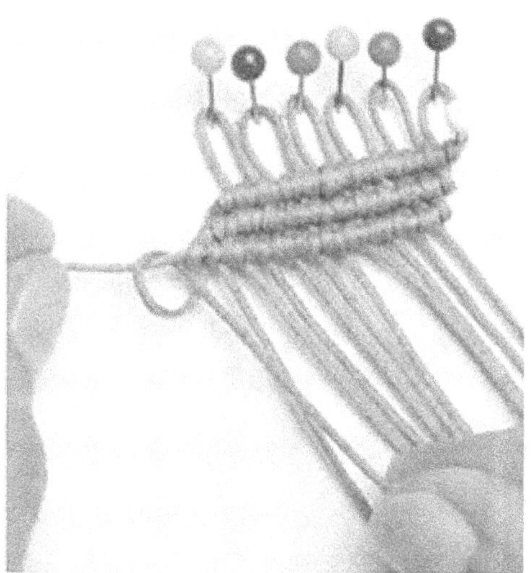

3. To change the direction to create a piece of macramé that zigzags, take the current core cord and pin it back across the vertical cords towards the right-hand side. Repeat steps 1 and 2, but now taking the next left-hand cord across to work each row.

- **HALF-HITCH VARIATIONS**

Half-hitch ribs can be worked at an angle for a diagonal pattern, and they can even be used to create shapes such as leaves and petals. While most macramé techniques use the double half-hitch, it is possible to create knotted designs using single half-hitches too (see Endless Falls).

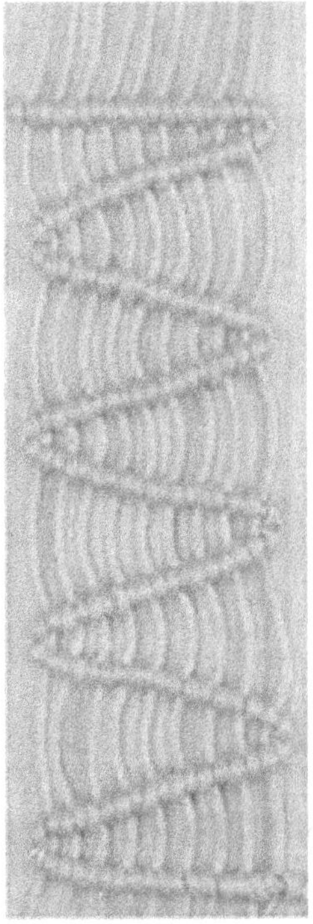

✓ **Diagonal half-hitch**

When making a horizontal rib the core cord is pinned straight across, but if the core cord is pinned at an angle, a diagonal rib will be created.

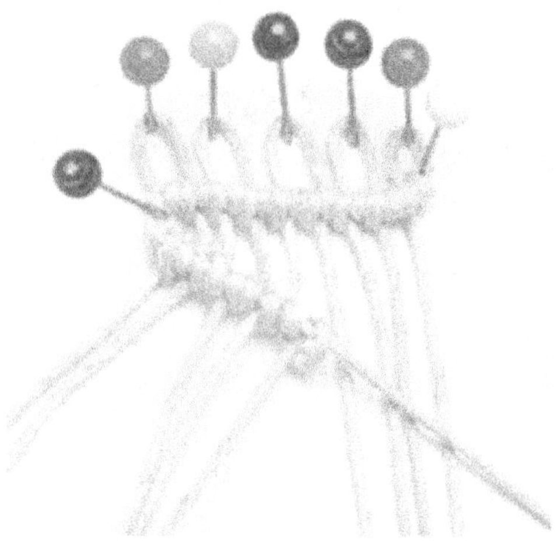

1. Work one row of half-hitch rib across the cords. Insert a pin at the end of the rib. Wrap the side (core) cord around the pin and across the vertical cord at the angle you want to create. Insert a pin to secure the core cord.

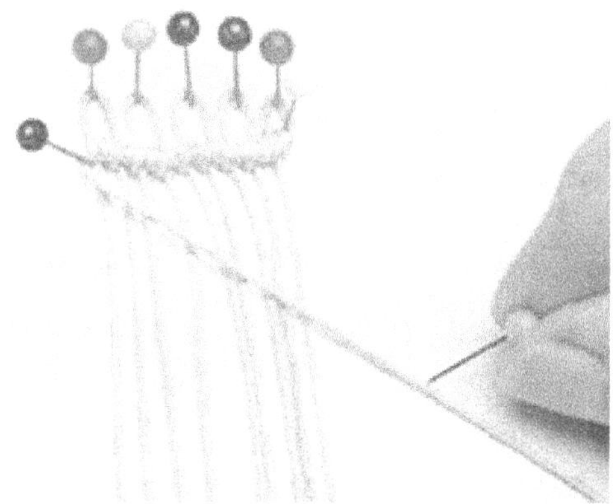

2. Tie two half-hitches with each vertical cord in turn making sure you keep the diagonal line of the rib as you firm up the knots. Make sure the vertical cords above the diagonal rib are not too loose or tight, and are lying flat.

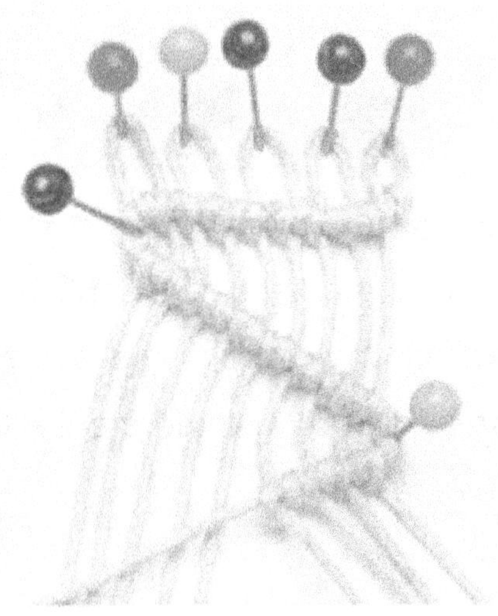

3 To create a zigzag simply pin the core cord diagonally in the opposite direction and work half-hitches with all the vertical cords again. At the end of the row goes back in the opposite direction once more, using the same core cord.

✓ **Petal shapes**

With a little forethought, half-hitch ribs may be used to make a variety of basic shapes. The angle of the rib and the spacing have produced a petal shape here; check out other designs for this technique.

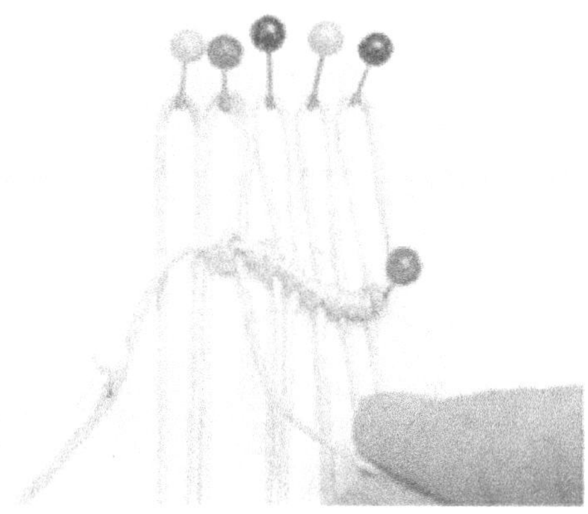

2. Pin the right-hand core cord, then cross it over the vertical cords and pin it so that the core cord has a gentle upwards curve. Make half-hitches all the way down the rope, changing each knot to keep the curve.

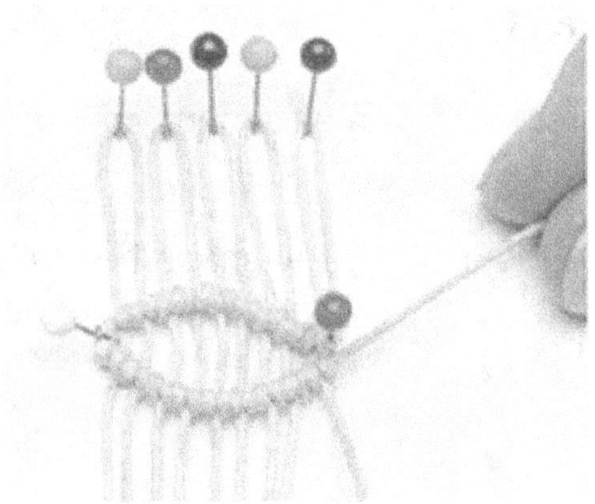

2. To create the petal shape, bend the central cord on the left around a pin and around the vertical cords in a downwards curve. To finish the petal formation, tie half-hitches over the centre thread.

CHAPTER FOUR

Macramé Home Projects

1. Projects 1: Macramé DIY Feathers

Lovely, feathery macramé feathers have recently clogged up our social media pages, but we're not complaining. They're stunning, and we've added them to our list of items to purchase and put in the kids' room. Yet, of course, we were all intrigued to see how they were made. How do you get the world's most wonderful soft fringe? Okay, we've now had the answers, which necessitates the use of a cat brush. Plenty was said. However, the possibilities are endless here, and we can't wait to see more of this process. In the meanwhile, we hope we'll inspire you to make these at home.

Materials:

- ✓ Cat brush

- ✓ 5mm single twist cotton string

- ✓ Sharp fabric shears

- ✓ Ruler

- ✓ Fabric stiffener

- ✓ For a med sized feather, cut:

- ✓ Strand for the spine (1 32" piece)

- ✓ Strands for the top (10-12 14" pieces)

- ✓ Strands for the middle (8-10 12" pieces)

- ✓ Strands for the bottom (6-8 10" pieces)

• Fold the 32-inch strand in two. Fold one of the 14-inch strands in two, then strap it under the spine.

• Fold a 14-inch strand in half and insert it into the top straight strand loop. Drag it across and horizontally position it on top of the opposite strand.

• Using the top string, drag the lower strands all the way through. This is the tie you'll be wearing.

• Pull all ends close closely. The beginning side will be rotated to the next page. As a consequence, if you first place the horizontal strand from left to right, you can then place the second horizontal strand from right to left.

• Lie under the first bent strand's spine and insert the folded strand into its circle. Drag the top circle through the strands on the bottom. Then cinch it up.

• Keep on working and function down in scale steadily.

• To stabilise the strands, grab the base of the middle (spine) strand with one hand and pull the strands up with the other. Pull the fringe back until it reaches the bottom of the middle strand, then stop.

• So, will you give it a tough finish? This not only helps to guide the structure, but it also smooths out the strands. To be honest, the strands that are smaller are preferable. It's also a good idea to invest in a good pair of cloth shears.

• After a hard scrub, place the feather on a sturdy surface since the cording can need to be brushed off with an animal brush. Since the brush will kill any poor or wood sheet, we suggest using a self-healing slicing pad or a flat piece of cardboard.

• Begin brushing at the spine and work your way deep into the String. Many hard strokes are needed to achieve the fine, smooth fringe.

• Make your way back. When brushing the bottom of the

spine, have the base of the spine in mind.

• You don't want the brush to yank any of your hair down. The feather would then be stiffened. The stitch is so fragile that picking it up and deciding where to put it would just cause it to flop. Give it a spray bottle and wait at least a couple of hours to begin.

Once the feather has stiffened a bit, you should go back and give it one more rinse. We believe this is the most difficult move. Keep it easy. It's better to make fewer cuts than it is to make more. You'll need to change the trim depending on how fast you shift the piece. When you've done cutting, apply another strip of fabric stiffener to the mix for good measure.

3. Projects 2: DIY Macramé Bottle Hanger

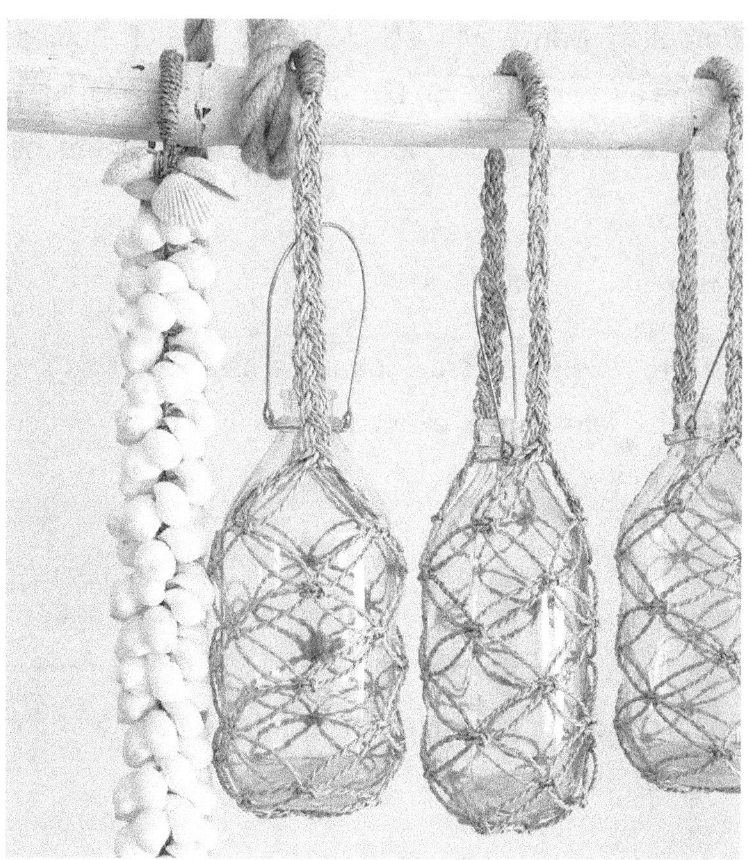

Materials:

- ✓ The Jars

- ✓ Macramé Cording

- ✓ Scissors

Do you have five minutes? That is exactly what will be

needed.

One thing to bear in mind, which might seem obvious, but we'll mention it anyway: we'll clean our yoghurt bottles and delete the stickers. Though our goo is securely stored, we're planning to use a little nice to get rid of all the sticker remnants.

"Troubles of renovation."

• 1st Step: weigh the cords. It can be as short or as long as you want. Here is the exact formula we used, which we found on Pinterest. '

Hanger length multiplied by two + jar length multiplied by ten inches We're going to go for 18 inches for the length of our hanger, so we double-checked it with String, then applied it to the height of our container, then attached about 10 inches and cut our String there.

We'll see that this duration is much more than enough.

• 2nd Step: After you've cut the first bit of ribbon, cut three more of the same size for a total of four pieces of the same thread.

• Third Step: The cords are bent in half. Tie a knot in the upper portion of the fold. This would be the cute little hanger portion. Tidy up the knot by pulling on the strings until it is straight and tidy.

• 4th Step: Tie it around a doorknob, cabinet knob, or other item. We found it much easier to tie the knots when it was hanging.

• 5th Step: Take two cords and tie a pair of knots with them. Do this for each of them before you do something else. Create knots all the way around as well.

• 6th Step: Right now. Taking one of those knots, two of the knots they just made, grab one rope, and tie those cords together with another knot.

Return until you have 4 knots. Assuring that they are both comparable. That's the second degree of knots, and the hanger is beginning to take shape.

Through you, this is a flashlight moment.

• 7th Step: Repeat the 6th step, but this time add a third row for knots. For these tiny jars to be the finest, we'll consider three lines of knots.

• 8th Step: Carry the little container inside and make sure it stays there. If it doesn't, make small modifications or stretch the knots out as far as possible.

If it looks good in there, simply tie a large knot at the bottom with all the loose threads. This fantastic knot will serve as the container hanger's foundation.

• 9th Step: Trim or leave the extra hang, which is mainly from the knot. Use fairy lights to fill your jar. Now is the time to put them up and feel it.

It's over.

What a beautiful pair they'll be.

You should hang them from your outside umbrella. We hung them with our tree, and it looked great.

These would be perfect for those friendly get-togethers you're planning.

Suspend them from the rooftop in a children's space for a boho look. It would make a truly fun little night light if you have some dimmer fairy lights.

4. Projects 3: Micro Macramé Christmas Decorations.

Materials:

- ✓ Cord/string macramé
- ✓ Scissors
- ✓ Twigs

✓ Tape masking

✓ Comb or hairbrush

✓ To the Twig Having the Cords Attached

• To begin, cut a small twig and tie six cords together with the lark's head knot. We'll use a cord, but we'll unwind it until we've tied it to the twig and changed it from three plies to one. Any chord must be at least 2 feet long.

• How to tie a four-phase head knot for larks To bind a lark's head knot, fold the rope in half and then lay it over the top of the twig in the middle.

• Bend the loop around the back of the twig and then draw the two ends together. There is a strong attraction. Rep on all six strings.

• A little macramé decoration with sparkle lights in a white Christmas theme.

• Christmas Square Knot Little Macramé Decoration

1st Square Knot

• It is time to begin the first line, 3 square knots until the strings are on the twig. Four cords connect those knots, and that the first four cords come from the left and split them.

• In four steps, how and when to attach a square knot for macramé. To create the square knot, bring it out of the upper left cord, so it appears like a number 4 pattern is developing.

• The first cord's ends are then tucked under a fourth cord.

• Then, at the end of the 4th chord, draw up from behind the middle two chords, through the space between the 1st and 2nd cords that looks like the four.

• Raise the ends of the first and fourth cords to reinforce and move the knot to the tip. It's the first half of a square knot.

At Macramé College, you'll learn how to tie a square knot.

• The second half of a square knot should be used in the same way, but in the opposite direction. But for the "4" reversed on the right side, you can make the "4" shape for the first and fourth cords.

• Then draw the first cord over the fourth.

• After that, feed the first cord tail underneath the second and third cords and up through the "4" type opening.

• Draw the first and fourth cords' edges together to tighten, and you'll get the first square knot.

1- 3rd row

• Macramé steps for attaching a square knot continue to work in four-cord sections. Attach a different square knot and then another square knot to make 3 along the top row.

• In segment two, you'll just tie two square knots. To do this, start by breaking the first one into cords. The first four cords of the second square knot are in row 2, followed by another. However, it will leave another two cords uncovered.

• A square knot may be formed by using just the middle four cords of a line for the third line.

• If you feel that you need to shift the tension, try to keep the knots evenly distributed and tightened.

4-5th row

• A piece of macramé with tiny square knots fixed to a table

• For row four, replicate row two with two square knots on both sides, cutting all two strings.

• For row 5, please replicate row 1 of three square knots.

6 Row Half Knot Hitch

• How do you tie a four-factor half hitch? You may finish this decoration with square knots or add a series of half hitch knots.

• Do a half hitch knot with the first cord in the chain, then pull horizontally across the piece. The lead rope is going to be it.

• Put the second cord behind and over a lead, through the loophole you've built. Repeat the knot with the second cord in a similar manner. It's just half of a hitch.

• Go down the rest of the cords, being careful not to bend the lead cord flat by drawing it horizontally over the other cords behind it.

• Tighten the knots by pushing on the lead rope.

5. Projects 4: Wall Hanging DIY Bohemian Macramé Mirror

Materials:

- ✓ Cording Macramé: 4mm

- ✓ Sharp Scissors (also available at JoAnn Fabrics)

- ✓ Ring of wood: 2 inches

- ✓ Wood Beads: 25millimeters Hole Size w/10mm

- ✓ With Sharp Scissors

- ✓ Wood Beads: 25millimeters Hole Size w/10mm

Instructions:

• Split the 4 pieces of macramé cord into 108-inch parts.

Mirror, mirror Larks Head Knot in Macramé

• Fold the pieces in half and tie them all together with a Lark's Head knot in the wood ring. Closely and tightly wrap the knots around each other. Break the Lark's Head links in half and tie them together in a square knot.

Model of a square knot macramé mirror

• Make two square knots with your hands.

• Begin by tying two square knots into two additional Lark's Head knots.

Macramé square knot in mirror

• When you begin the second square knot line, bring one of the other two square knots' edges together to form one large long square knot.

• Make seven square knots, going down either side and absolutely.

The square knot of the macramé keeper

• Cut the ends of the knots after they've been tied. two

strings on one line or two strings on both lines In the middle, there are four strings. Add tape to the cord's endpoints to conceal the broken ends. This would make it easier to add the beads. Congratulations for your achievement. This has been the most complicated part. The rest is only tying easy knots and keeping track of the ends.

Introduce beads to the macramé

• Connect one bead to each of the two side cords' rows. Make the bead also by tying a cord on both sides underneath it. Tie a single or (Overhand Knot) about 1/14 inch below the beads with the centre of the four strings.

• White mirror with macramé, beaded mirror with macramé, plain knotted mirror with macramé

• Take one cord from the middle and attach it to the two cords on the ends. Build a knot with the three by wrapping them around each other on both sides. Attach the mirror to get even knot sizes. Add one of the mirror's three side cordings to the backend to hold it steady.

• Tie simple ties on all three side cords on the lower left and right of a mirror. Divide the three side cords once more. Place one on either side of the mirror's back to secure it in place, and tie two around the front of the mirror in a knot.

• Enter knots on the back of the macramé mirror, a quick

macramé mirror tactic Turn the mirror over and tie all of the strings together.

• Delete the front tie by switching the mirror back over it. Slip the back cords into the tie and tighten the knot. Cut the chord's edge to a length of about 14 inches. Fraying occurs as you pull the edges or remove the cording. To fluff the Thread, brush the edges with the brush's edges. Hang it up and take pleasure in it.

6. Projects 5: Hanging Basket

This basket-style hanger is a multi-functional piece that is equally at home when used as a plant hanger in the conservatory, as a craft caddy in your sewing room, or as a hanging fruit bowl in the kitchen. Alternating square knots create a beautiful net-like pattern for the basket enclosure.

Materials:

- ✓ 167m (553ft) length of 2.5mm (1⁄8in) rope

- ✓ 6cm (23⁄8in) metal ring

- ✓ Two 20cm (77⁄8in) cane rings

Knots & techniques:

- ✓ Wrapped Knot

- ✓ Square Knot Triple

- ✓ Half Hitch Alternating

- ✓ Square Knot Pattern

- ✓ Overhand Knot Wrapping a Ring

- ✓ Mounting Techniques

Preparation:

- ✓ Cut forty 4m (131⁄4ft) lengths of 2.5mm (1⁄8in) rope

- ✓ Cut three 2m (61⁄2ft) lengths of 2.5mm (1⁄8in) rope

- ✓ Cut one 1m (31⁄4ft) length of 2.5mm (1⁄8in) rope

Method:

1. Tie a 2m (612ft) length of rope around the 6cm (238) metal frame (see Wrapping a Ring).

2. Fold the forty 4m (1318)ft lengths of rope in half around the interior of the ring to attach them to the ring. (For more

information about how to get started, see Mounting Techniques.)

3. Secure all cords together directly under the ring with a 3.5cm (138in) wrapped knot using one of the 2m (612ft) lengths of rope (see Wrapped Knot).

4. Divide the cords into eight groups of ten cords immediately under the wrapped knot. Each team will now form a sinnet (see Knotting Terminology). With each sinnet, repeat steps 5–8.

5. On either hand, tie four 10-cord square knots with four filler cords and three working cords (see Square Knot).

6. Drop down 17cm (634in) and tie one 6-cord square knot with four filler cords and one working cord on either side using the middle six cords.

7. Alternate cords (see Knotting Terminology) and tie two 5-cord square knots, one on either line, using three filler cords and one working cord.

8. Directly under, tie another 6-cord square knot for the middle six strings, using four filler cords and one working cord on each hand.

9. Lower yourself to 17cm (634in) and tuck all of your cords into the first of your cane loops. The holdings cord will now

be made out of the horizontal cane band (see Knotting Terminology). Attach each rope to the cane ring with triple half hitches (see Half Hitch Knots).

10. Tie a series of twenty square knots immediately under the first cane ring to protect it.

11. Drop 1.5cm (58in) down, alternating strings, and tie a second row of twenty square knots.

12. Work another eight rows in an alternating square knot pattern (see Alternating Square Knot Pattern).

13. Tuck all of the cords into the second cane loop. The horizontally placed cane ring will now act as the retaining cord. On the cane ring, tie triple half hitches with each rope.

14. Closely gather the rope and draw it upwards until it is level with the cane ring. This will serve as the hanging basket's core. Using the 1m (314ft) length of rope, tie a double overhand knot (see Overhand Knot).

15. Tie a 3.5cm (138in) wrapped knot over the top of the double overhand knot with the remaining 2m (612ft) of rope.

16. Cut the cords to the size you want.

7. Projects 6: Table Mat

This macramé table mat has a simple charm that is sure to please, from family breakfasts to dinner dates with friends. Create a package for trendy placemats or use only one to highlight your table centrepiece. The alternating half knot pattern produces a thick cloth that protects your table top, and these mats can be hand-washed if made from cotton rope.

Materials:

- ✓ 82.1m (272ft) length of 5mm (1⁄4in) rope

Knots & techniques:

- ✓ Horizontal Double Half Hitch

- ✓ Half Knot

- ✓ Overhand Knot

- ✓ Mounting Techniques

- ✓ Fraying

Preparation:

- ✓ Cut thirty-six 2.25m (71⁄2ft) lengths of 5mm (1⁄4in) rope

- ✓ Cut two 55cm (22in) lengths of 5mm (1⁄4in) rope

Method:

1. Use T-pins or adhesive tape to secure one of the 55cm (22in) rope lengths to a project board or a flat surface. (For more information about how to get started, see Mounting Techniques.) This will act as your keeping thread (see Knotting Terminology).

2. Use horizontal double half hitches (see Half Hitch Knots) to attach the 36 2.25m (712ft) lengths of rope to the holding string, leaving cord ends 10cm (4in) above the holding cord

to make the fringe.

3. Make a series of nine half knots directly under the row of double half hitches (see Half Knot).

4. Alternate cords and tie another row of eight half knots (see Knotting Terminology).

5. Alternate cords and tie nine half knots in a series.

6. Work another forty-eight rows in an alternating half knot pattern.

7. To make a second holding string, put the remaining 55cm (22in) length of rope directly under the last row of half knots and on top of both ropes. With horizontal double half hitches, tie both cables to the second holding string.

8. At either end of the two holding strings, tie an overhand knot (see Overhand Knot).

9. To make a fringe at either end of the mat, trim all cords to 5cm (2in) and fray (see Fraying).

7. Projects 7: Table Runner

For daily family meals to special event entertaining, such as weddings, this table runner makes a lovely statement piece to show off your table setting. The central diamond is formed using an increasing and diminishing square knot pattern, and the side panels can be conveniently lengthened to suit your table. The table runner may be hand-washed or spot-cleaned when made with cotton rope.

Materials:

- ✓ 208m (682½ft) length of 5mm (¼in) rope

- ✓ 50cm (20in) length of 2.5cm (1in) dowel

Knots & Techniques:

- ✓ Reverse Lark's Head Knot

- ✓ Square Knot

- ✓ Half Knot

- ✓ Alternating Square Knot Pattern

- ✓ Increasing Square Knot Pattern

- ✓ Decreasing Square Knot Pattern

- ✓ Mounting Techniques

- ✓ Numbering Cords

Preparation:

- Cut twenty-six 8m (26¼ft) lengths of 5mm (¼in) rope

Method

1. Using reverse lark's head knots to connect all twenty-six 8m (2614) rope lengths to the dowel, meaning that the rope lengths are equally spaced apart (see Reverse Lark's Head Knot). The mounted rope should be 36cm (141.18in) wide. (For more information about how to get started, see Mounting Techniques.)

2. Drop down 10cm (4in) and tie thirteen square knots in a row (see Square Knot).

3. Alternate cords (see Knotting Terminology) and tie a series of twelve half knots directly under the row of square knots (see Half Knot).

4. Alternate cords and tie thirteen half knots in a series.

5. Alternate cords and tie twelve half knots in a series.

6. Make a row of thirteen square knots directly underneath.

7. Alternate cords and tie a row of twelve square knots 3cm (118in) down.

8. Function another three rows in an alternating square knot pattern (see Alternating Square Knot Pattern) with 3cm (118in) gaps.

9. Go over steps 3–6 again.

10. Count the cords from 1 to 52. (see Numbering Cords).

11. Drop down 3cm (118in) and tie a square knot with cords 1–4. These cords can now be strung together to form a sinnet (see Knotting Terminology). Make six more square knots with 3cm (118in) gaps between them.

12. Repeat steps 11–12 for cords 49–52 this time.

13. Gather cords 25–28 and tie a square knot 3cm (118in)

deep.

14. Beginning with the square knot generated in step 13 with cords 25–28, work an increasing square knot pattern (see Increasing Square Knot Pattern), tying the rows directly underneath one another. Continue the rising square knot pattern until you've made eleven square knots in a row: this is the final row of the increasing square knot pattern.

15. Start a decreasing square knot pattern (see Decreasing Square Knot Pattern) directly underneath the row of eleven square knots before you have finished the last row of just one square knot.

16. Make a series of thirteen square knots 3cm (118in) deep.

17. Go over steps 3–8 again.

18. Go over steps 3–6 again.

19. Cut the chord ends to 12cm (434in) below the last square knot row.

20. Remove the mounted rope from the dowel with care. Cut the strings at the fold of the reverse lark's head knots. If required, trim the cord ends to fit the fringe at the other end of the runner.

8. Projects 8: Basic Plant Hanger

What better way to show any lovely greenery in your kitchen

or living room than with a macramé plant hanger? This easy pattern is an excellent place to begin learning how to make hanging homes for your houseplants. Replace your flowerpots with a favourite vase and fill it with new, hand-picked blooms for a fresh twist on this enduring classic.

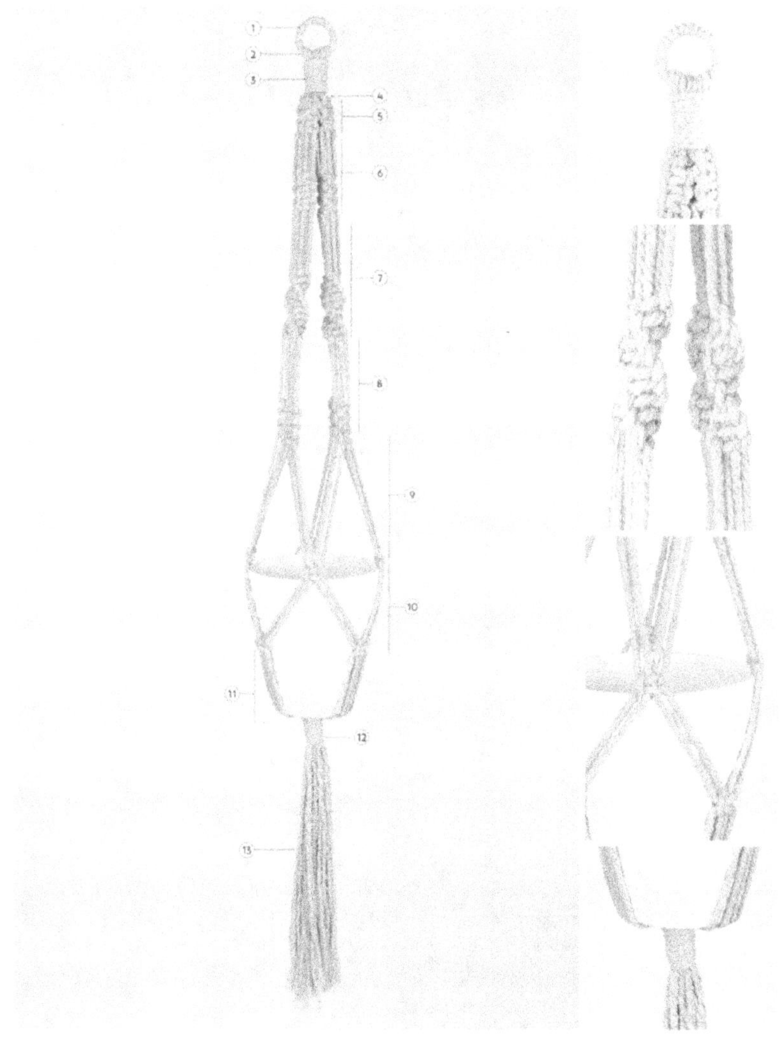

Materials:

- ✓ 43m (142ft) length of 5mm (1⁄4in) rope

- ✓ 4.5cm (13⁄4in) metal ring

- ✓ 30cm (1ft) length of 2.5mm (1⁄8in) cotton twine

Knots and Techniques:

- ✓ Wrapped Knot

- ✓ Square Knot

- ✓ Half Knot Spiral

- ✓ Overhand Knot

- ✓ Wrapping a Ring

- ✓ Mounting Techniques

- ✓ Fraying

Preparation:

- ✓ Cut eight 5m (161⁄2ft) lengths of 5mm (1⁄4in) rope

- ✓ Cut three 1m (31⁄4ft) lengths of 5mm (1⁄4in) rope

Method

1. Wrap a 1m (314ft) length of rope around the 4.5cm (134in) metal frame (see Wrapping a Ring).

2. Fold the eight 5m (1612ft) rope lengths in half around the inside of the ring to attach them to the ring. (For more

information about how to get started, see Mounting Techniques.)

3. Tie all of the cords together directly under the ring with a 4cm (112in) wrapped knot using a 1m (314ft) length of rope (see Wrapped Knot).

4. Divide the cords into four groups of four cords directly under the wrapped knot. Each community is now a sinnet (see Knotting Terminology). With each sinnet, repeat steps 5–8.

5. Make three square knots in a row (see Square Knot).

6. Tie three more square knots at a distance of 5cm (2in).

7. Tie a half knot spiral of ten half knots at a height of 7cm (234in) (see Half Knot Spiral).

8. Tie three square knots at a distance of 7cm (234in).

9. Drop down 13cm (518in). Bring two cords from each adjacent sinnet together and tie one square knot to alternate cords.

10. Drop down 9cm (31⁄2in). Bring two cords from each neighbouring sinnet together and tie one square knot to alternate cords.

11. Drop down 13cm (51⁄8in). Using the 30cm (1ft) length of cotton twine, tie all the cords together tightly and secure with

an overhand knot (see Overhand Knot).

12. Wrap the cotton twine in a 4cm (112in) wrapped knot with the remaining 1m (314ft) of rope.

13. Cut cords to 30cm (1ft) in length and fray.

9. Projects 9: Macramé Curtain

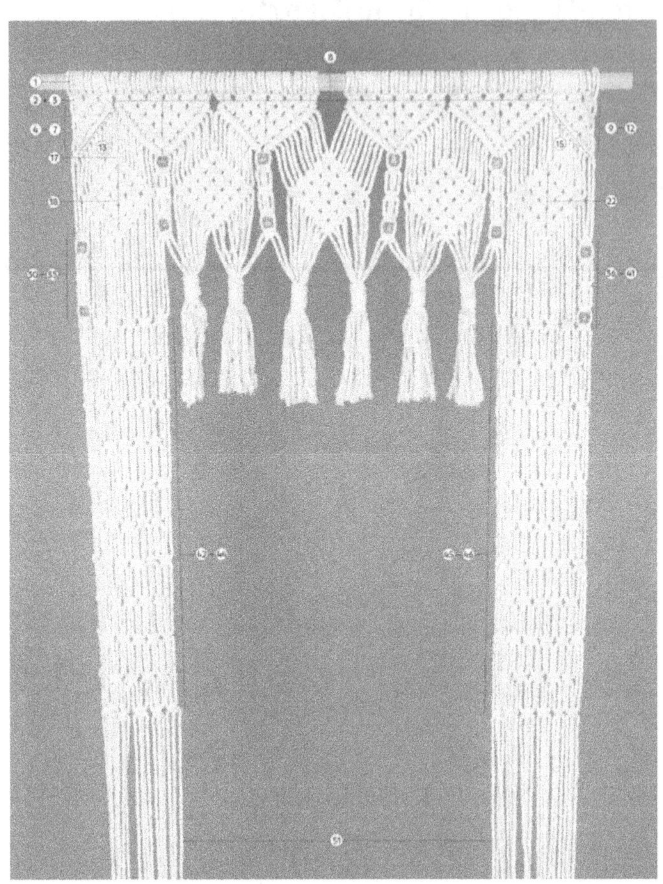

Materials:

- ✓ Rope

- ✓ Wooden dowel / curtain rod

- ✓ Masking tape

✓ Scissors

Instructions:

• On the foam core board, connect the four strands together and secure them with pins in the top node and the bottom of the two middle strands.

• On the west, take the outer right strand (pink) and cross it over the other two strands. Push the yellow outer left strand under the pink strand, between the middle strands, and over the pink strand on the other line.

• Pull the two threads together. You're clearly going to do the opposite of what you did in the first step! Place the outermost left strand (now the blue one) over the middle of the two strands. Shift the yellow strand from the outermost right strand under the pink line, between the two middle strands, and over the blue on the other side. Pull these two fibres together until they form a knot with the previous stage's threads. It's the most complicated part of all! The remaining measures would simply replicate these simple movements.

• Replicate steps 1-3 with four additional strands to make a knot identical to the first. Establish a new group with the two strands to the left of the second knot and the two strands to the right of the first knot.

• For the new team, duplicate the original knot by placing the outer right (purple) strand to the left over the middle of the two strands. Push the green outer left beach under the purple sea, behind the middle shore, and over the purple beach on the other side.

• Pull the two threads together. Now, reverse the first move! Place the outermost left strand (now red) over the middle of two strands. Pass the green strand under the purple, behind the two middle threads, and over the purple on the other line. Bring the two threads together.

• Move the two leftmost strands to the left and the two rightmost strands to the right to split the middle community of strands. Rep the basic node for all classes, and continue in this manner until you've done as many rows as you want. I made 14 groups of strings, each with four threads, all 100 inches high, before starting on the actual curtain. I found a clever knot at the top of the curtain and used it to cut two strands of rope twice the length needed (so 200 inches), then hang the strands over the rod at the centre point and tighten the knot to create a group of four strands.

• You'll notice that this is essentially the same concept as the yarn stage's simple knots, but on a much larger scale. I simply tied a simple knot at the top of each of the 14 pairs, then tied another row of knots below and between them (like in the yarn instructions). Then I went down another row and placed the knots under the initial knots, repeating the rows of knots until I had completed the required number of rows. When tying the links, make sure to take a step back and shape them into straight rows. I kept the ruler handy in case I needed to double-check the distance between each node in a row and the wooden curtain rod. I let the remaining threads hang down to finish the curtain as soon as I finished five rows of links. Hang your new curtain in the perfect location until you've done braiding the cords. To come to a halt, add masking tape (or other white tape; I used "dorm tape") to the ends of the rope where it meets the floor (my curtain is 6 1/2 feet tall). Break the tape, leaving about 2/3 to 1/2 of it on the cord. This will prevent the ends from fraying over night.

10. Project 10: Macramé brooch

Macramé is commonly thought of as a crude chunky knotting technique, but when done with fine strings, it becomes very elegant micro macramé. To create a rainbow effect across this pretty brooch, select matching colours.

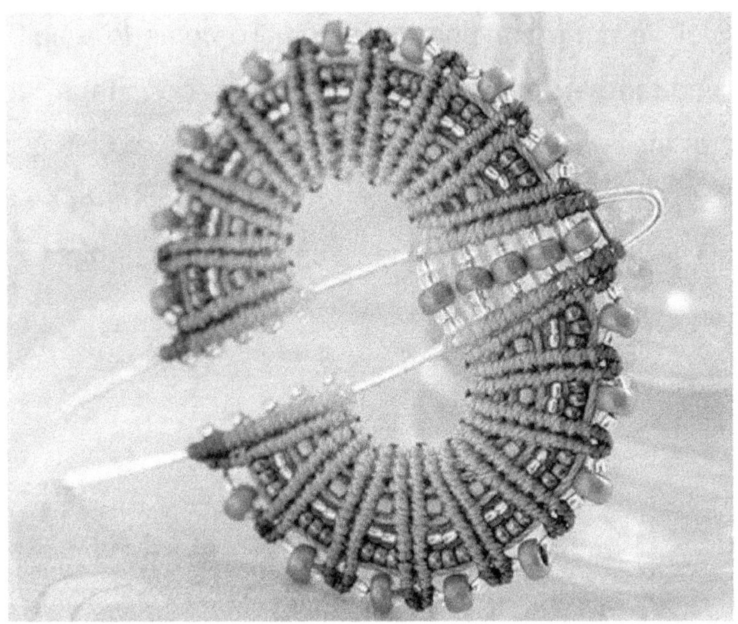

Materials

- ✓ 1.5m each of Superlon™ cord in purple, lilac, coral, light grey and dusky pink

- ✓ 20cm (8in) of 1mm (19swg) half hard sterling silver wire

- ✓ Seed beads: size 6 (3.5mm) matte silver, size 10 (2mm) colourlined peach, size 11 (2.2mm) silver-lined crystal and emeraldraspberry gold lustre

- ✓ Ultra suede™ 10cm (4in) square

- ✓ Brooch back

- ✓ Jewellery tools

- ✓ Needle and thread

- ✓ Foam core board

- ✓ Map pins

- ✓ Adhesive tape

- ✓ Spring clip (optional)

Instructions

1. Fold the silver wire in half to produce a 'V' shape with a slightly circular top.

Prepare the Superlon™ cords by arranging them in the following order: purple, lilac, coral, light grey, and dusky pink.

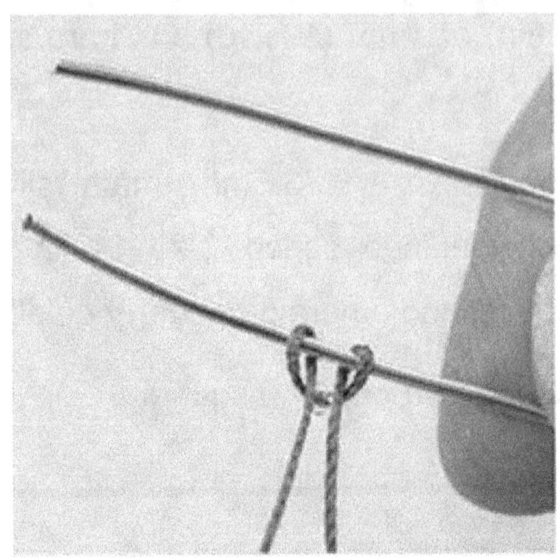

2. Drop a silver-lined crystal seed bead to the centre of the purple chain. Fold the cord in half and put it on one side of the 'V' over the cable. To make a verse lark's head knot, cross the tails over the wire and back through the circle (see Knotting Basics: Tying Basic Knots)

3. On either foot, work a half-hitch (see Knotting Basics: Tying Simple Knots). Rep steps 2–3 for the remaining coloured strings, each time inserting a bead.

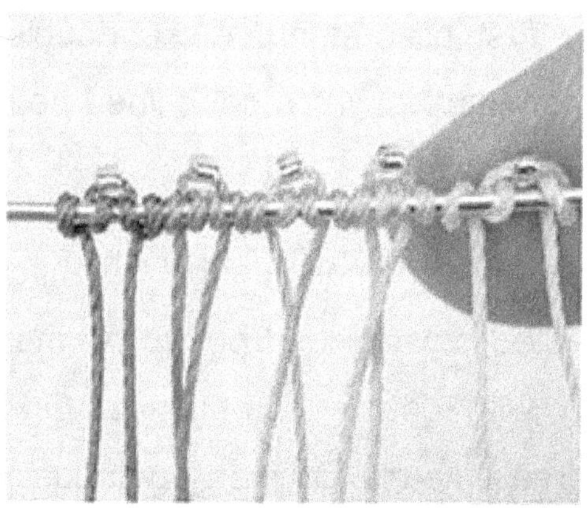

4. Put the wire shape on the foam core board and secure it with tape. Put the purple rope over the wire in a straight line. Working each chord in turn, make a double half-hitch (see Multi-strand Macramé: Straight Half-hitch Rib).

5. Place a map pin at the rib's end, then gently pull the purple cord back over the vertical cords at an angle. Use tape or a spring clip to keep it in place. With the dusky pink

cords and the first grey string, make double half-hitches. Work double half-hitches with a color-lined peach seed bead on the next grey thread.

6. On the first coral cord, make double half-hitches, then pick up two silver-lined crystal seed beads on the second coral cord and lock with double half-hitches. On the first lilac thread, add three emerald raspberry gold lustre seed beads and secure with double half-hitches once more.

7. Finish the remaining purple string with a silver-lined crystal, a size 6 matte silver, and a silver-lined crystal before working double half-hitches on the next lilac cord. Conduct the last double half-hitch.

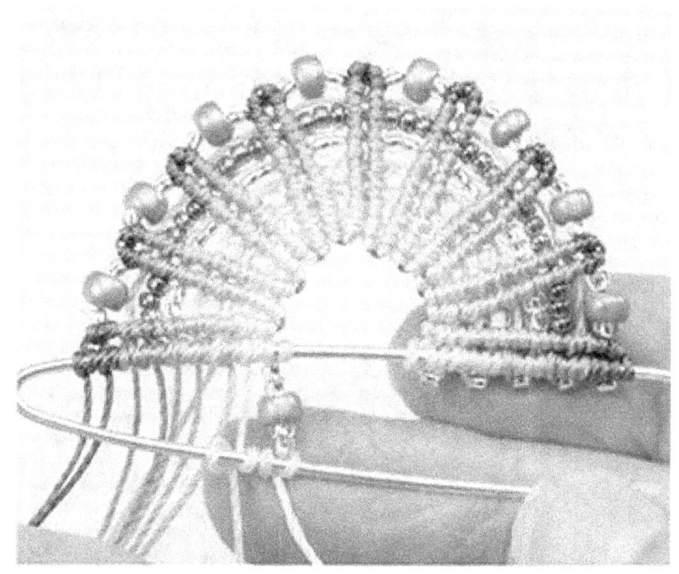

8. Repeat steps 1–6 or 7 before the macramé semicircle bends around to touch the wire again, depending on the stress. Return to the outside edge with the purple cord and work a smooth half-hitch rib.

Over the cable, work double half-hitches for each chord in turn.

9. Tuck the rope tails all the way behind the silver cable. On the first dusky pink cord, pick up two silver-lined crystals, a size 6 matte silver seed bead, and two silver-lined crystals. On the other side of the wire 'V' formation, make a double half-hitch. Connect the next dusky pink cord to the previous

one, but without the beads.

10. Repeat on the two grey strings, then work down the cable, beginning with the first colour and decreasing the number of silver-lined beads as the distance between the wires narrows.

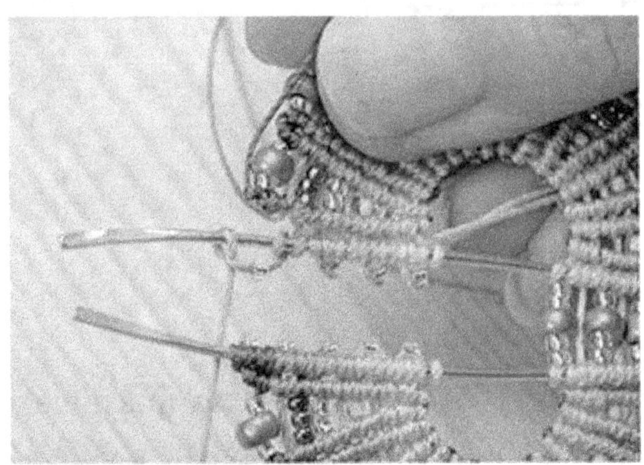

11. In macramé, make a semicircle to balance the first line, finishing with a straight half-hitch rib. For the first cord, make a double half-hitch and add a silver-lined crystal. To hold the bead, work another double half-hitch with the same thread. Rep with each additional cord.

12. Thread the cord ends invisibly with small stitches over the back of the macramé. Trim the edges clean. Cut UltrasuedeTM to match each semicircle and thread around

the edge invisibly.

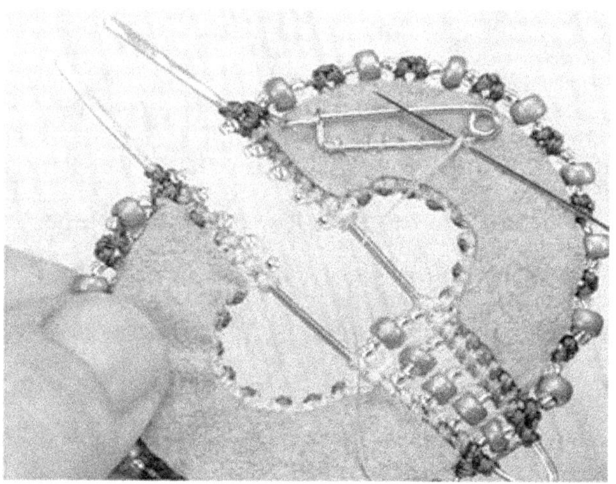

13. Sew a brooch back on one side on the reverse, sewing straight through to the right side and then back through to the reverse to hide the small thread between the macramé knots. Sew the ends together tightly.

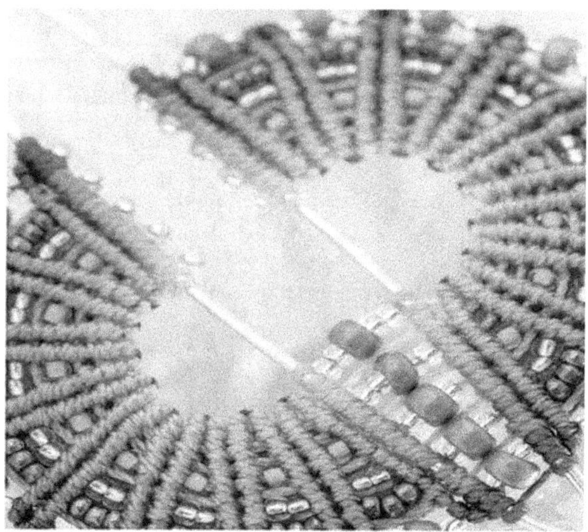

CHAPTER FIVE

The Most Effective Method To Macramé

There are various tools available to those who want to learn how to Macramé. Macramé is an art form that focuses on creating complex knots that create complete examples that can also be transformed into elegant bracelets, flower boxes, and decorative wall hangings. If you're interested in learning how to Macramé, the first and simplest step is to learn the simple knots and a couple of diagrams.

My next book, "Macramé Patterns" is a safe place to start looking for details about how to Macramé. Visual manuals are a huge support and can make learning how to macramé a breeze. Many people find it much easier to follow diagrams rather than formal orders, which can be difficult to understand. Also, after you've gotten used to the visual guides, it's time to get the materials you'll need to launch the Macramé process.

Looking at a map, regardless of how thorough and well-explained it is, isn't going to help you Macramé properly. To be able to Macramé efficiently, you must first have the string. Attempting to learn how to Macramé, like all other acquired skill, necessitates practise. To begin, gather some unmistakable, prepared depictions of simple diagrams. The less complex ones would tend to be less confusing than the dynamics of modern ones. With a lot of time and practise, you'll be able to advance into them.

Aside from the simple knot patterns, you'll be able to centre and train for a while before remembering the exercises and making symmetrical knots. If you're in a hurry and need to work out how to Macramé step by step, this won't be helpful. When you've finished the main knot systems, begin to organise them to construct required works, such as bracelets. Apart from knots, you'll also need an eye for matching the right colours to draw out the knot works.

Wristbands are ideal for beginners because they only require the most basic knots and do not require a high degree of intricacy. When you're getting more secure in your skills, you'll be able to manage incredibly good examples. The great thing about mind-boggling and very perplexing proposals is that they can only be created to deliver elaborate tasks that are unheard of.

The time it will take you to learn how to Macramé will be decided by a number of variables, including how easily you can pick up the technique. Since there are certain similarities in the techniques, whether you've been knitting or sewing for a while, the difficulty level should be fundamentally lower.

• Macramé Amateur

There are an infinite number of ways to learn a new talent or art, just as there are in life. I won't want to be an expert in Macramé. I am an utter novice. I'm just going to take you on my path to show you one way to do it, starting from one beginner and moving on to the next.

I'll provide you with all of the resources you'll need to figure out how to master Macramé in your own unique way. The best thing is that you don't have to be a professional to create stunning stylistic layout items for your house. It seems to be a lot more difficult than it is. Let's get started in this manner.

• First and foremost, practise How to Make a Macramé Bracelet

What makes you think it's a good idea to train first? This project, like most others, will cost you some money. How much is it? My first'real' project cost me about $30 in macramé cord (or macramé string, as it is often referred to) and a few dollars in wooden dowel.

Furthermore, you won't be able to buy macramé cord or macramé cord at Hobby Lobby or Michael's. You'll have to make arrangements for it (more on that later). If you're like me and like to start a project the day you finally say to yourself, "I need to start this," I recommend starting with a training project.

I found a "Easy Macramé Tutorial" on YouTube and started my first, smaller-than-expected project. YouTube is full with knots of amateur macramé creations and instructional lessons.

• Today's Macramé

The shade palette of today's macramé has been modified. If anyone is purposely emulating the 1970s to fit their retro shag cover, it's normally made up of each colouring in turn, with white, pastels, or earth tones being the most common. In any case, that isn't exactly accurate; macramé can be rendered in a number of designs. It's mostly lovely knotwork.

When people check our web for "macramé line," we at Paracord Planet are a little shocked. We sell numerous styles of making wire. Cotton and hemp rope was once believed to be safe. However, those were just the rules at the day, and everything went.

Manufactured filaments, including paracord, are widely used in its recent revival. Cotton rope, engineered to make a cord, manila/hemp rope, jute, and even calfskin are used in other macramé lines. A macramé rope can be made out of any cable. I'm sure that at some point in the future, the cutting edge will look at modern macramé and wonder how we could ever imagine that anything so hideous will ever be beautiful, just as we did to our parents.

It's easy to get started with macramé. It's a wide category of production, so everyone can find something in the pastime that fits their tastes.

CONCLUSION

Macramé's charm as a retro art style that has survived centuries of extinction and thrived as a technique of choice for designing basic yet elegant pieces is truly unrivalled. The fact that you've opted to read this manual suggests that you're well on your way to building something amazing. There is an undeniable sense of accomplishment that comes with creating your own masterpiece, and by reading this novel, you have taken the first step toward achieving the euphoria.

Macramé can also be used as a starting point for your dream small company. After you've perfected your Macramé skills, you can easily sell your items and get a good price for them, particularly if you can make items like bracelets that people purchase frequently. You might also teach people how to make bespoke Macramé fashion accessories and start your own small business. Macramé gives an almost infinite range of possibilities.

Do not throw this book out until you've finished reading it. Using that as a starting point, and search for more in-depth materials both online and offline to help you develop your skills. This book discusses simple knots and projects for beginners, but you won't be a beginner for long if you practise Macramé on a daily basis. Macramé, as previously mentioned, can be very soothing, and it is an excellent way to get family and friends together. You should show your loved ones any of these simple knots and direct them to this carefully planned beginner's guide to Macramé, as you've learned here.

The maxim "Practice makes better" is the most significant rule in Macramé. Your talents are likely to deteriorate with time if you avoid training on a daily basis. So keep your talents sharp, flex your artistic muscles, and continue to make mind-blowing handmade masterpieces. Jewelry and fashion accessories made with even the simplest Macramé knots are still stunning, making them ideal presents for loved ones on special occasions. Giving someone a Macramé bracelet, for example, sends the message that you not only remembered to buy them a gift, but that you really value them so much that you want to devote your time in creating something beautiful just for them, and believe me, that is a strong message. The most appealing aspect of Macramé, though, is that it aids in the creation of long-lasting products. As a consequence, you can keep a piece of furniture or a fashion accessory that you designed for yourself for many years, admire its beauty, and always feel nostalgic whenever you recall when you made it. It's much cooler if you co-created the item with someone else. Macramé accessories are also excellent gifts because of their versatility.

Macramé can also be used as a starting point for your dream small company. After you've perfected your Macramé skills, you can easily sell your items and get a good price for them, particularly if you can make items like bracelets that people purchase frequently. You might also teach people how to make bespoke Macramé fashion accessories and start your own small business. Macramé gives an almost infinite range of possibilities.

So stay focused, keep learning, and keep improving. Hello, and welcome to a world of limitless possibilities!

Let me thank you for reading my guide. There are a number of great books on the topic, so I really appreciate you choosing my guide. If you enjoyed the book, I'd like to ask for a small favor. I'd love for you to take a couple of minutes to leave a review for this book on Amazon. Your feedback will help me to make improvements to this guide!